BANANA BREADS, LOAF CAKES
& OTHER QUICK BAKES

BANANA BREADS, LOAF CAKES & OTHER QUICK BAKES

60 deliciously easy recipes for home baking

RYLAND PETERS & SMALL

Designers Toni Kay and Paul Stradling
Editor Gillian Haslam
Head of Production Patricia Harrington
Creative Director Leslie Harrington
Editorial Director Julia Charles

First published in 2021.
This revised edition published in 2025
by Ryland Peters & Small
20–21 Jockey's Fields
London WC1R 4BW
and
1452 Davis Bugg Road
Warrenton, NC 27589

www.rylandpeters.com
email: euregulations@rylandpeters.com

10 9 8 7 6 5 4 3 2 1

Recipe collection compiled by Julia Charles.

Text © Kiki Bee, Susannah Blake, Clare Burnet, Maxine
Clark, Linda Collister, Megan Davies, Julian Day, Amy
Ruth Finegold, Mat Follas, Tonia George, Victoria Glass,
Dunja Gulin, Victoria Hall, Tori Haschka, Lola's
Cupcakes, Claire & Lucy McDonald, Hannah Miles,
Miisa Mink, Suzy Pelta, Isidora Popovic, Sarah Randall,
Annie Rigg, Shelagh Ryan, Wendy Sweetser & Ryland
Peters & Small 2021.
Design and photographs © Ryland Peters & Small 2021
(see page 144 for photo credits).

ISBN: 978-1-78879-689-7

A CIP record for this book is available from the
British Library.
US Library of Congress Cataloging-in-Publication Data
has been applied for.

The authorised representative in the EEA is
Authorised Rep Compliance Ltd,
Ground Floor, 71 Lower Baggot Street,
Dublin, D02 P593, Ireland.
www.arccompliance.com

Printed and bound in China.

Notes

• Both British (metric) and American (imperial
plus US cups) are included in these recipes for
your convenience; however it is important to work
with one set of measurements and not alternate
between the two within a recipe.

• All spoon measurements are level unless
otherwise specified.

• All eggs are medium (UK) or large (US), unless
otherwise specified. Uncooked or partially cooked
eggs should not be served to the very old, frail,
young children, pregnant women or those with
compromised immune systems.

• When a recipe calls for the grated zest of citrus
fruit, buy unwaxed fruit and wash well before
using. If you can only find treated fruit, scrub well
in warm soapy water before using.

• Ovens should be preheated to the specified
temperatures. We recommend using an oven
thermometer. If using a fan-assisted oven, adjust
temperatures according to the manufacturer's
instructions.

Contents

Introduction

Banana bread is one of those classic bakes, a timeless recipe in nearly every baker's repertoire. But did you know there are endless variations on the basic recipe? In the pages that follow you will find so many ideas to ring the changes – from adding nuts or chocolate chips, to flavouring with passion fruit, coffee or peanut butter, or serving with raspberry labne. So next time you find an over-ripe bunch of bananas in the fruit bowl, experiment with a different recipe.

This book also includes many other mouthwatering recipes for loaf cakes. There's a stunning oatbake topped with blueberries and raspberries, a lemon loaf with white chocolate frosting, an indulgent sticky toffee ginger loaf, even a loaf cake delicately flavoured with lavender.

The tea breads chapter will introduce you to lots of new ways of baking with dried fruit. Try the mulled wine and cranberry tea bread, the sticky marzipan and cherry loaf or the apricot and nut loaf. If small bakes appeal to you, there are plenty of ideas for muffins and mini cakes, and the book finishes with a tempting selection of bundt cakes and scones, including mini blueberry bundts, pear and blackberry scone round, crunchy prune and vanilla custard brioche cakes and a gooey chocolate Scandinavian kladdaka. Throughout the book you will also find recipes for vegan and gluten-free bakes, so no one needs to miss out on these tempting treats.

Whether you are baking for a special occasion, looking for quick bakes for weekday lunch boxes or searching for new ideas for breakfast and afternoon tea, you are sure to find inspiration in these delicious recipes.

Happy baking!

Chapter 1
Banana breads

Classic banana bread

There is something very comforting about a slice of banana cake. Sticky and full of flavour, yet not too sweet. Try your hardest to wait for the cake to cool down before you eat it, but we forgive you if you can't resist the temptation! This banana bread keeps really well in an airtight container and can even be toasted and served with butter.

3 large very ripe bananas
1 teaspoon bicarbonate of soda/
   baking soda
50 ml/3½ tablespoons full-fat/
   whole milk
115 g/1 stick butter, softened,
   plus extra for greasing
115 g/½ cup plus 1 tablespoon
   caster/granulated sugar
2 eggs
190 g/1½ cups minus 1 tablespoon
   self-raising/self-rising flour,
   sifted

*900-g/2-lb. loaf pan, greased and
lined with parchment paper*

MAKES 1 LOAF CAKE

Preheat the oven to 160°C (325°F) Gas 3.

Peel and mash the bananas with a fork until you have a mixture that is a combination of smooth banana and small chunks; you do not want it too smooth. Set aside until needed.

In a small bowl, mix the bicarbonate of soda/baking soda with the milk and stir until dissolved. Set aside.

Place the butter and sugar into the bowl of a stand mixer fitted with the paddle attachment (or use a hand-held electric whisk and a large mixing bowl) and beat on medium speed until blended. This will take a minute or so.

Slowly add the eggs, one at a time, on low speed, stopping to scrape down the bowl occasionally. Once the eggs have been incorporated, add the mashed bananas and mix. With the speed on low, slowly add the flour and the milk mixture, a little at a time, alternating between the two, until all the ingredients have been incorporated and the mixture is fully combined.

Pour the batter into the prepared loaf pan and bake in the preheated oven for 45–50 minutes or until golden brown and a skewer inserted into the centre of the cake comes out clean or with just a few crumbs attached. Leave the cake to cool completely in the pan before turning out and serving.

Banana & passion fruit loaf

Passion fruit bring another level of flavour to a classic banana bread, and the dried banana slices added as decoration add a pleasing crunch.

225 g/1¾ cups self-raising/
   self-rising flour
½ teaspoon bicarbonate of soda/
   baking soda
100 g/7 tablespoons butter,
   softened and cubed, plus extra
   for greasing
175 g/¾ cup plus 2 tablespoons
   caster/granulated sugar
2 large UK/extra large US eggs,
   lightly beaten
3 passion fruit
3 very ripe bananas, mashed

TO DECORATE
100 g/¾ cup icing/confectioner's
   sugar
1 passion fruit
dried banana slices

*450-g/1-lb. loaf pan, greased and
   lined with parchment paper*

MAKES 1 LOAF CAKE

Preheat the oven to 180°C (350°F) Gas 4.

Sift the flour and bicarbonate of soda/baking soda into a bowl. Put the butter and sugar into the bowl of a stand mixer (or use a hand-held electric whisk and a large mixing bowl) and beat until pale and fluffy. Add the beaten eggs and sifted flour mixture alternately to the bowl.

Halve the passion fruit and scoop out the pulp into a sieve/strainer over a bowl. Using a teaspoon, press and stir the pulp to extract the juice. Discard the leftover seeds. Add the passion fruit pulp and mashed banana to the cake mixture and mix again.

Tip the mixture into the prepared loaf pan and spread it evenly with a spatula. Bake in the preheated oven for 55 minutes, or until golden and risen and a skewer inserted into the centre comes out clean. Leave to cool in the pan.

To decorate, sift the icing/confectioner's sugar into a small bowl. Halve the passion fruit and scoop out the pulp into the bowl – no need to sieve the pulp this time. Mix together with a teaspoon. The icing/confectioner's sugar will seem stiff at first, but persevere until it is thoroughly mixed. If the glaze still seems a little thick, add a drop or two of cold water – the consistency of the glaze will depend on the size of the passion fruit and how ripe it is. You want the glaze to be a thick, spreadable consistency.

Tip the cold loaf out of the pan and peel off the paper. Spoon the glaze over the top of the loaf and decorate with dried banana slices. Leave to set for about 30 minutes before slicing.

Chocolate chip banana bread

This is a cake that can't go wrong, unless you are not patient enough to wait for the bananas to completely over-ripen — they have to be black to get that deep flavour. The chocolate chips are really just gilding the lily, but when they come out molten and oozy, they make the bread utterly irresistible (and feel free to add more than the amount specified below if you are feeling really decadent!).

225 g/1¾ cups plain/all-purpose flour
1 teaspoon baking powder
½ teaspoon salt
175 g/¾ cup packed light brown sugar
4 very ripe bananas, mashed
85 g/5½ tablespoons butter, melted, plus extra for greasing
2 large UK/extra large US eggs, lightly beaten
100 g/⅔ cup chopped dark/bittersweet chocolate

900-g/2-lb. loaf pan, greased and lined with parchment paper

MAKES 1 LOAF CAKE

Preheat the oven to 180°C (350°F) Gas 4.

Put the flour, baking powder and salt in a mixing bowl and set aside. In another bowl, mix the sugar and bananas until there are no large lumps, then beat in the butter and eggs.

Tip the wet ingredients into the dry ingredients and mix, being careful not to overmix otherwise the bread will be tough. Stir in the chocolate. Spoon the thick batter into the prepared loaf pan and bake in the middle of the preheated oven for 40–45 minutes, until a skewer inserted into the middle comes out clean.

Let the bread cool in the pan for 10 minutes, then turn out onto a wire rack to cool completely. When cold, serve in slices with butter or a decadent dollop of ricotta.

Chocolate, yogurt & banana tea bread

This is a real treat for children everywhere or the big kid that lurks in all of us. If making this for children, milk chocolate and a flavoured yogurt make a great combination, or for adults try really dark chocolate and natural yogurt. This really does improve with keeping — even for a day, if you are able to keep your hands off it.

55 g/4 tablespoons unsalted butter, softened, plus extra or greasing
150 g/¾ cup soft light brown sugar
2 large eggs, beaten
100 g/½ cup natural, banana or chocolate yogurt
3 very ripe bananas, mashed
300 g/2¼ cups self-raising/self-rising flour
½ teaspoon salt
200 g/7 oz. dark/bittersweet chocolate (60–70% cocoa solids) or milk chocolate (over 32% cocoa solids), grated
chocolate and hazelnut spread, to serve (optional)

2 x 450-g/1-lb. loaf pans, greased and lined with parchment paper

MAKES 2 LOAF CAKES

Preheat the oven to 180°C (350°F) Gas 4.

Using a hand-held electric whisk, beat the butter and sugar together in a large mixing bowl until well mixed (it won't look very creamy). Gradually whisk in the eggs, little by little, then the yogurt, and finally stir in the mashed bananas. Fold in the flour and salt, then the grated chocolate. Spoon into the prepared loaf pans and smooth the surface.

Bake in the preheated oven for about 35 minutes, or until risen and firm and a skewer inserted into the centre comes out clean. The loaves will crack on the top. Remove from the oven and leave to cool in the pan for 10 minutes. Turn out onto a wire rack and leave to cool completely.

Store in an airtight container for 1 day to mature before serving in thick slices with chocolate and hazelnut spread if you're feeling particularly indulgent!

Latte banana bread

A cup of coffee and a slice of banana bread — how many mornings have been made by this coupling? So, in the spirit of efficiency, here the two components come together as one. Here the coffee tempers the candy sweetness of ripe bananas, lacing the bread with a note of caramel and the milky coffee keeps the bread moist and cake-like.

110 g/7 tablespoons soft butter, plus extra for greasing
300 g/2⅓ cups plain/all-purpose flour
1 teaspoon bicarbonate of soda/baking soda
1 teaspoon salt
125 g/⅔ cup granulated sugar
2 eggs
4 very ripe bananas, mashed
85 ml/⅓ cup milky coffee (1 shot of espresso topped up with milk)

900-g/2-lb. loaf pan, greased and lined with parchment paper

MAKES 1 LOAF CAKE

Preheat the oven to 180°C (350°F) Gas 4.

Sift the flour, bicarbonate of soda/baking soda and salt into a large mixing bowl.

In a separate bowl, use a hand-held electric whisk to beat the butter and sugar together until light and fluffy.

Add the eggs, mashed bananas and coffee to the butter and sugar mixture and stir well. Fold in the flour mixture. Do this gently; you don't want to overwork the flour and have it turn out tough.

Tip the mixture into the prepared loaf pan. Bake in the preheated oven for about 1 hour, or until well risen and golden brown and a skewer inserted into the centre comes out clean. Remove from the oven and allow to cool in the pan for a few minutes, then turn out onto a wire rack to cool further before serving.

Serve with a coffee on the side, and perhaps with some ricotta or butter over the top.

Banana & walnut bread

This is such a flexible recipe too; you can use dried fruit in place of the walnuts or even just leave it plain. Slice and serve spread with butter, or try it toasted for a tasty change at breakfast.

1 large or 2 small very ripe
  bananas
40 g/3 tablespoons salted butter,
  softened, plus extra for
  greasing
100 g/¾ cup self-raising/
  self-rising flour
70 g/⅓ cup caster/granulated
  sugar
a pinch of salt
1 egg
100 g/⅔ cup chopped walnuts

*450-g/1-lb. loaf pan, greased and
  lined with parchment paper*

MAKES 1 LOAF CAKE

Preheat the oven to 150°C (300°F) Gas 2.

In a large bowl, mash the banana with a fork. Add the butter, flour, sugar and salt and stir together. Add the egg, followed by the walnuts, and beat into the mixture. This can also be done with an electric stand mixer or a hand-held electric whisk.

Spoon the mixture into the prepared loaf pan, spread level and bake in the preheated oven for 45 minutes or until a skewer inserted into the middle of the loaf comes out clean.

This loaf is best eaten within a day or 2 of baking, but will keep for up to 4 days in an airtight container.

Gluten-free banana & brazil nut bread

The addition of brazil nuts gives this gluten-free loaf cake a lovely texture, but you can substitute any nuts you prefer — pistachios or hazelnuts both work well. This recipe makes two loaves, so make one to eat today and one for the freezer.

2 very ripe bananas
115 g/1 stick butter, softened, plus extra for greasing
115 g/½ cup plus 1 tablespoon caster/granulated sugar
2 large UK/extra large US eggs
115 g/1 scant cup gluten-free self-raising/self-rising flour OR 115 g/1 scant cup gluten-free all-purpose baking flour plus 1 teaspoon baking powder and ¼ teaspoon xanthan gum
3 tablespoons buttermilk
2 teaspoons ground cinnamon
1 teaspoon ground mixed spice/ apple pie spice
100 g/1 cup brazil nuts, coarsely chopped

CARAMEL GLAZE
1 tablespoon butter
1 tablespoon light soft brown sugar
1 tablespoon golden/light corn syrup
¼ teaspoon fine sea salt

2 x 450-g/1-lb. loaf pans, greased and lined with parchment paper

MAKES 2 LOAF CAKES

Preheat the oven to 180°C (350°F) Gas 4.

Put the bananas in a bowl and mash with a fork. Put the butter and sugar in a mixing bowl and whisk until light and creamy. Add the eggs one at a time, whisking after each addition. Add the mashed banana, flour, buttermilk, cinnamon, mixed spice/apple pie spice and brazil nuts and fold in until everything is incorporated.

Divide the batter between the prepared loaf pans and bake in the preheated oven for 25–30 minutes, until the cakes are firm to the touch and a skewer inserted in the middle of each cake comes out clean. Remove the loaves from the oven and let cool slightly while you make the glaze.

To make the salted caramel glaze, gently heat the butter, sugar, syrup and salt in a saucepan until the butter has melted and the sugar dissolved. Drizzle the caramel over the warm cakes to glaze and leave for a few minutes before turning out onto a wire rack to cool.

These cakes will keep for up to 3 days if stored in an airtight container. They also freeze very well, so if you don't need both cakes, you can freeze one for up to 2 months.

Banana bread with raspberry labne

For an indulgent start to the day, try banana bread with this beautiful raspberry labne. Labne is a strained yogurt which has a consistency somewhere between cream cheese and yogurt. The longer you leave it, the firmer it becomes so play around with the consistency.

125 g/1 stick unsalted butter, softened, plus extra for greasing
250 g/1¼ cups caster/ granulated sugar
2 large UK/extra large US eggs, beaten
1 teaspoon vanilla extract
250g/2 cups plain/all-purpose flour
2 teaspoons baking powder
4 very ripe bananas, mashed

RASPBERRY LABNE
150 g/1 generous cup fresh or frozen raspberries
100 g/½ cup caster/granulated sugar
500 g/2 cups Greek yogurt
1 teaspoon vanilla extract

900-g/2-lb loaf pan, greased and lined with parchment paper
2 fine mesh sieves/strainers, one lined with several layers of muslin/cheesecloth

MAKES 1 LOAF CAKE

First make the raspberry labne, as this needs to strain for up to 24 hours. Place 50 g/½ cup of the raspberries in a small saucepan with the sugar and 100 ml/scant ½ cup of water. Set over a gentle heat and simmer until it reduces by one-third. Remove from the heat and strain through the unlined sieve/strainer set over a mixing bowl. Discard the raspberry pulp, cover the syrup and set aside to cool completely.

Add the yogurt, cooled syrup, vanilla and remaining raspberries, and mix together. Pour the mixture into the lined sieve/strainer set over a mixing bowl. Draw the cloth together, twist the gathered cloth to form a tight ball and tie the ends with kitchen string. Suspend the wrapped labne over the bowl and set in the fridge for 12–24 hours.

Discard the drained water and transfer the labne to a bowl, ready to serve with the banana bread.

Preheat the oven to 180°C (350°F) Gas 4.

Beat the butter and sugar together in a large mixing bowl until light, fluffy and a pale cream colour. Gradually beat in the eggs, one at a time, before adding the vanilla. In a separate bowl, sift together the flour and baking powder.

Gently fold the mashed bananas into the wet mixture a little at a time, alternating with the sifted flour mixture so that the mixture doesn't split. Transfer the banana batter to the prepared loaf pan, then bake in the preheated oven for 20 minutes.

Reduce the oven temperature to 160°C (325°F) Gas 3 and cook for a further 40–45 minutes until golden brown, firm to the touch and a skewer inserted into the middle comes out clean. Set aside to cool in the pan for 5 minutes, then turn out onto a wire rack to cool completely. Cut into thick slices and spread with the raspberry labne.

Peanut butter banana bread

This banana bread uses a handful of salted peanuts as well as plenty of the crunchy kind of peanut butter which adds a little extra texture, but if you only have smooth, you can use that.

50 g/3½ tablespoons butter, plus extra for greasing
3 very ripe bananas, plus 1 extra for decoration
120 g/4½ oz. crunchy peanut butter
220 g/1⅔ cups plain/all-purpose flour
80 g/scant ½ cup caster/granulated sugar
100 g/½ cup soft light brown sugar
3 teaspoons baking powder
½ teaspoon sea salt
2 eggs
2 tablespoons salted peanuts

900-g/2-lb. loaf pan, greased and lined with parchment paper

MAKES 1 LOAF CAKE

Preheat the oven to 180°C fan/200°C/400°F/Gas 6.

Melt the butter in a small pan over a medium heat (or in a microwave), then remove from the heat.

Put the bananas in a bowl and mash well. Add the peanut butter and melted butter and mix well to combine.

Put the flour, both sugars, baking powder and salt into a separate, large bowl. It's worth sifting here to help avoid clumps in the brown sugar. Mix to combine, then make a loose well in the centre. Add the eggs and loosely whisk. Now pile the banana mix on top and gradually combine all the ingredients together in a whisking motion, starting with the wet mix in the well. Once all the ingredients are combined, transfer the batter to the prepared loaf pan.

Slice the remaining banana (in any way you like) and add to the top of the batter, along with the salted peanuts.

Bake in the preheated oven for 45–60 minutes, until risen and baked through and a skewer into the centre of the cake comes out clean.

Transfer the loaf pan to a cooling rack and let it sit for 15 minutes in the pan, then turn out and cool fully before slicing and serving.

Choc-chip banana bread in a jar

Sometimes it is fun to do something just because you can. This banana bread, baked in a jam jar, is a case in point. It is cake! In a jar!

2 very ripe bananas
110 g/1 stick butter
150 g/¾ cup caster/granulated sugar
2 eggs
225 g/1¾ cups self-raising/ self-rising flour
40 g/¼ cup chocolate chips (or any broken-up chocolate)

6 ovenproof glass jars

MAKES 6

Preheat the oven to 140°C (275°F) Gas 1.

Mash the bananas. Using a hand-held electric whisk, cream the butter and sugar together until a pale cream colour and fluffy. Add the eggs, then stir in the flour. Mix everything together well, then fold in the chocolate chips.

Divide the mixture between 6 sterilized jars. They need to be filled just over a third full. Make sure there is no mixture spilled on the sides. Place on a baking sheet and bake in the preheated oven for about 35–40 minutes. They will be done when they have risen to just below the top and when a skewer inserted into the centre comes out clean. Allow to cool, then, if you wish, screw the lids on and pack for a picnic!

Caramel banana mug cake

Caramel and banana are a match made in heaven in this oh-so-easy microwave cake which bakes in less than 3 minutes. For an extra treat, top with a dash of dark rum as soon as the cake comes out of the microwave.

1 very ripe banana
1 tablespoon porridge/rolled oats
¼ teaspoon ground cinnamon
a generous pinch of salt
1 egg
2 tablespoons light brown sugar
1 tablespoon vegetable oil
3 tablespoons self-raising/
    self-rising flour
2 tablespoons canned caramel/
    dulce de leche

TO SERVE
1 tablespoon dark rum (optional)
canned caramel/dulce de leche
banana slices
ground cinnamon

a large microwavable mug

MAKES 1

In a small bowl, mash the banana with a fork. Add the porridge oats, cinnamon and salt, and stir together.

Put the egg and sugar into the microwave-proof mug, then whisk together using a fork. Tip the banana mixture into the mug and mix well. Stir in the oil, then add the flour and mix thoroughly until you have a batter which will be lumpy because of the banana. Swirl in the caramel.

Place the mug on a microwave-proof plate in case any of the caramel overflows and microwave for 2 minutes 40 seconds at 800W. The cake will rise, then sink a little and should still be a little wet to touch.

As soon as the cake is out of the microwave, top with rum, if using. Either way, leave the mug cake to cool for 3 minutes because the caramel will be very hot. To serve, drizzle with caramel, top with slices of banana and dust with cinnamon.

Chapter 2
Loaf cakes

Chocolate & vanilla marble cake

When making a marble cake, the challenge is to keep the cake moist and to make each flavour distinctive. Experiment with different combinations to make fun colour mixes (raspberry and lime also looks amazing). Add a little extra milk to the chocolate sponge mix as cocoa will dry out a cake without some extra moisture to compensate. You ideally need a set of weighing scales for this recipe.

BASIC SPONGE
5 eggs
approx. 250 g/scant 2 cups
    self-raising/self-rising flour
approx. 250 ml/1 cup plus
    1 tablespoon vegetable oil,
    plus extra for greasing
approx. 250 g/1¼ cups caster/
    granulated sugar

VANILLA SPONGE
1 teaspoon vanilla extract

CHOCOLATE SPONGE
4 teaspoons unsweetened cocoa
    powder
50 ml/3½ tablespoons milk

900-g/2-lb. loaf pan, greased and
    lined with parchment paper

MAKES 1 LOAF CAKE

Preheat the oven to 140°C (280°F) Gas 1.

Place your mixing bowl onto your scales and zero the scales. Into the bowl, crack the eggs and make a note of the weight. Add the same weight of each of the flour, oil and sugar.

Mix for a few minutes with a hand-held electric whisk or in a stand mixer until it forms a smooth batter.

Divide the cake mixture equally between two mixing bowls. Fold the vanilla extract into one portion and fold the cocoa powder and milk into the other portion.

Now, alternating large spoonfuls of each mixture, dollop the sponge mixes into the prepared loaf pan until all the mixture has been used. Bake in the preheated oven for 70–90 minutes, until a skewer poked into the centre comes out clean.

Leave the cake to cool for 20 minutes before removing from the pan. Serve in thin slices.

Mocha swirl loaf with espresso icing

The fromage frais in this loaf keeps the fat content down, while the polenta gives it a lovely crunchy crust.

1 slightly rounded tablespoon espresso instant coffee powder
200 g/¾ cup fromage frais
75 g/½ cup polenta/cornmeal
125 g/1 stick butter, softened, plus extra for greasing
225 g/1 cup caster/granulated sugar
3 large UK/extra large US eggs
200 g/1⅔ cups self-raising/self-rising flour
½ teaspoon bicarbonate of soda/baking soda
1 teaspoon vanilla extract
2 teaspoons cocoa powder

ESPRESSO ICING
100 g/⅔ cup icing/confectioner's sugar
1 slightly rounded teaspoon espresso instant coffee powder

900-g/2-lb. loaf pan, greased and lined with parchment paper

MAKES 1 LOAF CAKE

Preheat the oven to 180°C (350°F) Gas 4.

Put the espresso powder in a cup with one tablespoon boiling water and stir to dissolve, then leave to cool.

Next, take a scant tablespoon from the fromage frais and set it aside for the icing/frosting. Put the remaining fromage frais into the bowl of a stand mixer with the polenta/cornmeal, butter, sugar, eggs, flour and bicarbonate of soda/baking soda (or use a large mixing bowl and a hand-held electric whisk) and beat until combined. Transfer half the mixture to another bowl. Stir the vanilla extract into the first bowl. Stir the dissolved coffee and the cocoa into the second bowl.

Spoon the 2 mixtures into the prepared loaf pan in 3 layers, alternating spoonfuls of each mixture in each layer to resemble a chequerboard. Finally, using a skewer, gently swirl the layers together a few times until you have a definite swirl pattern on top of the loaf.

Bake in the preheated oven for 55 minutes, or until risen and a skewer inserted into the centre comes out clean. Leave to cool in the pan.

To make the espresso icing/frosting, sift the icing/confectioner's sugar into a bowl and mix in the espresso powder along with the reserved tablespoon of fromage frais. Add enough cold water to make the icing a spreadable consistency – about 2 teaspoonfuls – but add it gradually, stirring, as you might not need it all.

Turn out the loaf from the pan and spread the icing on top. Leave to set before slicing.

Sticky toffee ginger loaf

Sometimes you can have your cake and pudding too. This moreish recipe combines two delicious desserts – sticky toffee pudding and ginger cake – into one decadent cake.

200 g/1⅓ cups pitted dates, halved
1 teaspoon bicarbonate of soda/
 baking soda
75 g/5 tablespoons unsalted butter,
 softened, plus extra for greasing
115 g/½ cup soft brown sugar
2 teaspoons ground ginger
3 eggs
80 g/½ cup (about 4 balls) stem
 ginger, finely chopped
225 g/1¾ cups self-raising/
 self-rising flour, sifted

CARAMEL GLAZE
110 g/½ cup caster/granulated
 sugar
40 g/3 tablespoons butter
225 ml/1 scant cup single/light
 cream

*900-g/2-lb. loaf pan, greased and
 lined with parchment paper*

MAKES 1 LOAF CAKE

Preheat the oven to 180°C (350°F) Gas 4.

Place the dates and bicarbonate of soda/baking soda in a large mixing bowl. Cover with 330 ml/1⅓ cups of boiling water. Stir and set aside for at least 20 minutes.

In a separate bowl, beat the butter and sugar together until thick and pale in colour. Add the ground ginger, then the eggs, one at a time, beating well after each addition.

Stir in the soaked date mixture, stem ginger and flour, and mix until well combined – the mixture should be quite loose.

Pour the batter into the prepared pan and bake in the preheated oven for 50–60 minutes, or until a skewer inserted into the centre comes out clean.

Remove from the oven and let the cake cool in the pan for 10 minutes, then turn out onto a wire rack to cool completely.

To make the caramel glaze, choose a saucepan large enough to ensure that the sugar is no more than 2 mm/⅛ inch thick over the base, otherwise the heat will not distribute evenly through the sugar. Set the pan over a gentle heat and add the sugar and 1 teaspoon of water. Shake the pan rather than stir it with a spoon to avoid the sugar hardening before it liquefies – this will take about 15 minutes and you want a deep, golden caramel. Remove from the heat and whisk in the butter until it has all melted and is well combined.

Heat the cream in a separate pan over a gentle heat, then whisk it into the caramel until smooth and glossy. Set aside to cool and firm up slightly so that it has a good spreading consistency.

Spread the glaze over the top of the cooled cake and serve in slices.

Oatbake with blueberries & raspberries

This is the perfect dessert for a weekend brunch. The fresh berries make it irresistible and not too heavy. Serve it with a dollop of whipped cream or a drizzle of custard if you think it needs a little something else.

100 g/¾ cup porridge/rolled oats
300 ml/1¼ cups hot milk
100 g/6½ tablespoons unsalted butter, at room temperature, plus extra for greasing
60 g/5 tablespoons caster/granulated sugar
50 ml/3 tablespoons runny honey
1 teaspoon vanilla extract
1 egg, lightly beaten
1 teaspoon baking powder
120 g/1 cup plain/all-purpose flour
150 g/1 generous cup blueberries
150 g/1 generous cup raspberries
icing/confectioner's sugar, for dusting

900-g/2-lb. loaf pan, greased and lined with parchment paper

MAKES 1 LOAF CAKE

Preheat the oven to 180°C (350°F) Gas 4.

Put the oats and hot milk in a mixing bowl and set aside for a few minutes to allow the oats to absorb most of the milk and to cool down slightly.

Put the butter and sugar in a separate bowl and cream with a wooden spoon or a hand-held electric whisk until pale and fluffy. Stir in the honey and vanilla extract. Gradually add the egg, a little at a time, beating well after each addition.

Sift the baking powder and flour together, then fold into the butter mixture. Drain any remaining liquid from the oats, then stir into the mixing bowl.

Pour the mixture into the prepared loaf pan and sprinkle the blueberries and raspberries evenly on top.

Bake in the preheated oven for 50–60 minutes, until a skewer inserted into the centre comes out clean. Leave to rest in the pan for 10 minutes before turning out onto a wire rack to cool. Dust with a little icing/confectioner's sugar before serving.

Castella cake

This Japanese sponge cake has a delightfully bouncy texture due to the gluten in the bread flour. It has a subtle honey flavour that goes so well with a cup of matcha green tea. The baked cake requires overnight chilling.

75 g/¼ cup runny honey
2½ tablespoons warm water
6 eggs
220 g/1 cup plus 1 tablespoon
   caster/granulated sugar
½ teaspoon vanilla extract
200 g/1½ cups white strong/bread
   flour, sifted twice

TO FINISH
1 tablespoon runny honey
½ tablespoon warm water

*900-g/2-lb. loaf pan, greased and
lined with parchment paper*

MAKES 1 LOAF CAKE

Preheat the oven to 160°C (325°F) Gas 3.

In a small bowl, whisk together the honey and warm water and set aside.

Place the eggs into the bowl of a stand mixer fitted with the whisk attachment (or use a hand-held electric whisk and a large mixing bowl) and whisk on high speed until combined and frothy. Add the sugar, then beat together on high speed for 5 minutes. You want to create a lot of volume in the eggs. The texture will be thick and the colour will be pale yellow.

Add the honey mixture into the egg mixture and whisk on low speed until combined. Add the flour gradually on low speed and beat until just combined, about 1 minute. Do not over-mix.

Pour the batter into the prepared loaf pan and gently tap on the work surface to remove large air bubbles. Bake in the preheated oven for 35–40 minutes or until golden brown and a skewer inserted into the centre comes out clean.

To finish, mix the honey and warm water in a bowl and brush the mixture over the top of the hot cake using a pastry brush. Allow to soak in for a minute or two.

Place a large sheet of clingfilm/plastic wrap on the work surface. Turn the cake out of the pan and place directly onto the clingfilm/plastic wrap, top down. Peel off the parchment paper. Immediately wrap the hot cake with clingfilm/plastic wrap and place in the fridge overnight. This will help the cake to stay moist and keep its shape.

Remove the cake from the fridge and unwrap when ready to serve. Cut into thick slices with a sharp bread knife and enjoy. You can also cut off the sides to expose the white interior if you want to serve this cake the traditional Japanese way.

Lemon loaf with white chocolate frosting

The rich, citrussy base and creamy white chocolate frosting are fabulously matched in this perfect teatime cake.

65 g/4 tablespoons unsalted butter, at room temperature, plus extra for greasing
135 g/⅔ cup golden caster/granulated sugar
2 eggs
135 g/1 cup plain/all-purpose flour
1½ teaspoons baking powder
finely grated zest and freshly squeezed juice of 2 lemons

WHITE CHOCOLATE FROSTING
150 g/5 oz. white chocolate, chopped, plus extra, grated, to decorate
75 ml/⅓ cup double/heavy cream

450-g/1-lb. loaf pan greased and lined with parchment paper

MAKES 1 LOAF CAKE

Preheat the oven to 170°C (325°F) Gas 3.

Put the butter and sugar in a mixing bowl and mix well using a hand-held electric whisk. Add the eggs and whisk for a couple of minutes until pale and fluffy. Gently fold in the flour and baking powder. Finally, stir in the lemon zest and juice until well mixed.

Pour the mixture into the prepared loaf pan and bake in the preheated oven for 25 minutes. When it's ready, the cake will be a rich golden colour and springy to the touch, and a skewer insert into the centre will come out clean. Remove it from the oven and turn out onto a wire rack to cool before frosting.

Meanwhile, make the white chocolate frosting. Put the chocolate in a mixing bowl. Put the cream in a saucepan and gently bring to the boil over a low heat, stirring frequently. Pour into the mixing bowl and whisk until you get a smooth cream. Leave to cool for a couple of minutes, then refrigerate for 15 minutes to stiffen.

Spread the frosting on top of the cake and sprinkle some grated chocolate over it.

Lemon drizzle loaf cake

Who can resist this intensely lemony loaf cake? It has long been a favourite at teatime and for very good reason, as the featherlight sponge is soaked in a deliciously tangy lemon syrup. Be warned, it is incredibly hard to stop at a single slice.

110 g/7 tablespoons butter, softened, plus extra for greasing
175 g/¾ cup plus 2 tablespoons caster/granulated sugar
175 g/1⅓ cups self-raising/self-rising flour, sifted
1 teaspoon baking powder
a pinch of salt
2 eggs
4 tablespoons whole/full-fat milk
finely grated zest of 2 lemons

TOPPING
100 g/½ cup caster/ granulated sugar
freshly squeezed juice of 2 lemons

900-g/2-lb. loaf pan, greased and lined with parchment paper

MAKES 1 LOAF CAKE

Preheat the oven to 180°C fan/200°C/400°F/Gas 6.

Put all the cake ingredients, except the lemon zest, into a large mixing bowl and, using a hand-held electric whisk, thoroughly combine until the mixture is creamy and has a dropping consistency. Fold through the lemon zest and pour the cake batter into the prepared pan. Level the top and bake for 30–35 minutes, or until a skewer inserted into the centre comes out clean.

In the meantime, stir the lemon juice and sugar together in a jug/pitcher to make the drizzle topping.

Once the cake has baked, remove it from the oven and stab it all over with a skewer to create lots of fine holes for the syrup to soak through. Pour the lemon syrup over the hot cake and leave the cake to cool completely in its pan on top of a wire rack, before turning out.

Gluten-free lemon & poppy seed drizzle loaf

Loaf cakes are slice well and their smaller size and simplicity means they are the perfect option for those 'just because' days when a bake seems essential, but there's no particular celebration in the offing.

240 ml/1 cup whole/full-fat milk
1 tablespoon sunflower oil
2 eggs
260 g/1¾ cups plain/all-purpose gluten-free flour
14 g/3½ teaspoons baking powder
¼ teaspoon salt
⅜ teaspoon xanthan gum
250 g/1¼ cups caster/granulated sugar
zest of 2 lemons
70 g/5 tablespoons unsalted butter, softened, plus extra for greasing
2 tablespoons poppy seeds
crème fraîche, to serve

GLAZE
freshly squeezed juice of 2 lemons
100 g/½ cup caster/granulated sugar

900-g/2-lb. loaf pan, greased and lined with parchment paper

MAKES 1 LOAF CAKE

Preheat the oven to 180°C (350°F) Gas 4.

In a jug/pitcher, combine the milk, oil and eggs.

Place the flour, baking powder, salt, xanthan gum, sugar, lemon zest and softened butter in the bowl of a stand mixer (or use a large mixing bowl and a hand-held electric whisk). Slowly mix the dry ingredients and butter until the mixture resembles fine breadcrumbs. Continue to mix on a slow speed and pour in the wet ingredients. Once combined, turn the speed to medium and mix for 3–5 minutes until the batter thickens. Add the poppy seeds and mix until evenly distributed. Pour the batter into the loaf pan and level the top.

Bake in the preheated oven for 40–45 minutes until it is risen, golden and springs back when pressed lightly on the top, and a skewer inserted into the centre comes out clean. Put the pan onto a wire rack and allow to rest for 1–2 minutes while you mix together the glaze.

Stir the lemon juice and sugar together in a bowl. Leave the cake in the pan and prick the surface all over with a fork or skewer. Pour over the glaze – it's important to do this while the cake is still warm. Leave the cake to cool completely in the pan on the wire rack, by which the time the glaze will have crystallized and set. Remove the loaf from the pan. Slice and serve, perhaps with a dollop of crème fraîche.

Cook's tip: You can ring the changes with other citrus fruits – an orange or lime version is just as delicious.

Iced orange seed cake

Seed cake dates from Victorian times, and early recipes always used caraway seeds. If you find the aniseed flavour of caraway too harsh, you could use poppy seeds or fennel seeds instead.

175 g/1½ sticks unsalted butter, softened, plus extra for greasing
175 g/1 scant cup unrefined golden caster/superfine sugar
finely grated zest of 1 orange
1 tablespoon caraway seeds
2 large UK/extra large US eggs, separated
175 g/1⅓ cups self-raising/self-rising flour
50 g/½ cup ground almonds
¼ teaspoon freshly grated nutmeg
2 tablespoons milk

FROSTING
75 g/½ cup icing/confectioner's sugar
about 2 tablespoons orange juice
orange food colouring

TO DECORATE
crystallized/candied orange peel (see Cook's tip, right)
caster/granulated sugar

900-g/2-lb. loaf pan, greased and lined with parchment paper

MAKES 1 LOAF CAKE

Preheat the oven to 350°F/180°C/gas mark 4.

Beat the butter and sugar together until pale and creamy. Stir in the grated orange zest, and caraway seeds, followed by the egg yolks, one at a time. Sift in the flour, and stir in with the ground almonds, nutmeg and milk.

Whisk the egg whites in a clean, grease-free bowl, until standing in firm peaks. Stir 1 tablespoon of the whites into the mixture to loosen it, then gently fold in the remainder using a large metal spoon. Spoon the mixture into the prepared loaf pan in an even layer and level the top. Bake in the preheated oven for 45–50 minutes, or until a skewer inserted into the centre comes out clean. Leave to cool in the pan for 30 minutes before turning out onto a wire rack to cool completely.

To make the frosting, sift the icing/confectioner's sugar into a bowl, and stir in enough orange juice to make a paste thick enough to coat the back of a spoon. Tint with a little orange food colouring, and drizzle or spread over the cake. Decorate with crystallized/candied orange peel, and leave to set.

Cook's tip: To make crystallized/candied orange peel, pare strips of peel from an orange using a vegetable peeler, taking care not to remove too much pith with the peel. Cut the strips into fine long shreds with a small sharp knife. Heat 115 g/generous ½ cup caster/granulated sugar in a pan with 100 ml/½ cup water, and, once the sugar has dissolved, add the orange peel. Simmer for 10–15 minutes, or until the peel becomes transparent. Drain well, and, using two forks, toss the peel in caster/superfine sugar until coated. Leave to cool before using to decorate the cake.

Lavender loaf

Lavender has been used for centuries as a flavouring for food, and it takes just a tiny amount to transform this simple cake into a delicately flavoured delight, perfect for summer eating.

130 g/1 stick plus 2 teaspoons salted butter, softened
130 g/⅔ cup caster/granulated sugar
2 eggs
grated zest of 1 lemon
35 g/3 tablespoons ground almonds
100 g/¾ cup plain/all-purpose flour
40 g/⅓ cup self-raising/self-rising flour
3 teaspoons dried lavender flowers (see Cook's tip, right)

450-g/1-lb. loaf pan, greased and lined with parchment paper

MAKES 1 LOAF CAKE

Preheat the oven to 170°C (325°F) Gas 3.

In a large bowl, cream the butter and sugar together until pale and fluffy. Add the eggs one at a time, beating between each addition. Add the lemon zest, ground almonds and both flours and beat to a smooth batter. Finally, add the lavender and stir through.

Spoon the mixture into the prepared loaf pan, spread the top level and bake in the preheated oven for 40 minutes or until a skewer inserted into the centre comes out clean. Leave to cool in the pan for 30 minutes before turning out onto a wire rack to cool completely.

This cake is best eaten on the day of baking, but will keep for up to 4 days in an airtight container or frozen for up to 2 months.

Cook's tip: If using home-grown lavender, be sure to wash it thoroughly and dry in a low oven. Alternatively, you can buy edible lavender online.

Cornish saffron cake

In medieval times saffron was a popular flavouring; its delicate strands giving doughs a rich golden hue. In England at that time, saffron was grown in Cornwall, where it was added to cakes made for special occasions. Saffron cakes and buns are still baked in that region today.

oil, for greasing
1 teaspoon saffron strands
2 tablespoons hot water
450 g/3¼ cups strong white bread flour, plus extra for kneading
½ teaspoon salt
5 teaspoons (2 × 7-g/¼-oz sachets) active dry yeast
150 g/1¼ sticks unsalted butter, diced
50 g/¼ cup unrefined golden caster/granulated sugar
200 g/1½ cups dried currants
50 g/⅜ cup chopped candied/mixed peel (see page 51 for how to make your own)
1 teaspoon ground cinnamon
½ teaspoon ground allspice
¼ teaspoon freshly grated nutmeg
2 large UK/extra large US eggs
115 ml/½ cup lukewarm milk

TO GLAZE
25 g/2 tablespoons unsalted butter, melted
25 g/2 tablespoons unrefined golden caster/granulated sugar

900-g/2-lb. loaf pan, greased and lined with parchment paper

MAKES ONE LOAF CAKE

Crumble the saffron strands into a small bowl and add the hot water. Leave to soak for 30 minutes.

Sift the flour and salt into a mixing bowl, and stir in the yeast. Rub in the butter until the mixture resembles fine breadcrumbs. Stir in the sugar, dried currants, candied peel, cinnamon, allspice and nutmeg.

Beat together the eggs and milk, then add to the dry ingredients along with the saffron and its soaking water. Stir to mix, then work everything together to make a dough. Transfer the dough to a lightly floured board and knead for about 10 minutes, or until it is smooth and elastic. Put the dough in a lightly greased bowl, cover with clingfilm/plastic wrap and leave in a warm place for 3–4 hours, or until doubled in size.

Knock the dough down, knead for 1–2 minutes, and then shape into a loaf. Put the dough in the prepared pan, seam side down, cover with a damp kitchen towel and leave to rise again for about 2 hours in a warm place, until the dough rises to the top of the pan.

Preheat the oven to 200°C (400°F) Gas 6. Bake the risen dough for 20 minutes. Reduce the oven temperature to 180°C (350°F) Gas 4, and bake for another 25–30 minutes, or until the base of the loaf sounds hollow when tapped.

Glaze the top of the loaf by brushing with the melted butter, and sprinkling over the sugar. Bake for an additional 3 minutes. Turn the loaf out onto a wire rack to cool, and serve cut into slices, spread with butter or clotted cream and jam.

Carrot loaf cake

Moist and wholesome with a pleasant sweetness, there's something honest and comforting about freshly-baked carrot cake.

150 g/¾ cup packed light brown soft sugar
1 egg
170 ml/¾ cup corn oil
140 g/1 cup plus 1½ tablespoons wholemeal/whole-wheat flour
½ teaspoon baking powder
1 teaspoon ground cinnamon
½ teaspoon freshly grated nutmeg
¼ teaspoon salt
1 ripe banana, mashed
50 g/⅓ cup chopped walnuts
30 g/3 tablespoons sultanas/golden raisins
125 g/⅔ cup grated carrots

TOPPING
100 g/scant ½ cup mascarpone
40 g/⅓ cup icing/confectioner's sugar
10 g/2 teaspoons salted butter, softened
a squeeze of fresh lemon or lime juice (optional)
grated lemon zest, to garnish

450-g/1-lb. loaf pan, greased and lined with parchment paper

MAKES 1 LOAF CAKE

Preheat the oven to 170°C (325°F) Gas 3.

Put the sugar, egg and corn oil in a large bowl and lightly beat together. Add the flour, baking powder, cinnamon, nutmeg and salt and stir to a smooth mixture. Add the mashed banana, walnuts and sultanas/golden raisins, followed by the carrot, and stir together.

Spoon the mixture into the prepared loaf pan and bake in the preheated oven for 55 minutes or until a skewer inserted into the centre comes out clean. Allow to cool in the pan for about 15 minutes, then turn out onto a wire rack to cool completely.

To make the topping, put the mascarpone, icing/confectioner's sugar and butter into a bowl and whisk until light and creamy. If desired, add a squeeze of lemon or lime juice to bring a bit of zing to the frosting. Spread the topping over the cake and decorate with lemon zest.

This cake will keep for 5–7 days in the fridge.

Vegan sweet potato pound cake

This vegan cake is studded with cubes of sweet potato, which have been steamed to soften them. When sweet potatoes aren't available, try using pumpkin or rhubarb in this recipe.

125 g/1 full cup peeled and cubed sweet potato
130 g/1 cup unbleached plain/all-purpose flour
65 g/½ cup plain wholemeal/whole-wheat flour
1 teaspoon bicarbonate of soda/baking soda
1 teaspoon baking powder
¼ teaspoon salt
100 g/½ cup raw/unrefined brown sugar
110 ml/½ cup sparkling mineral water
3 tablespoons apple concentrate (see Cook's tip for an alternative)
65 g/⅓ cup sunflower oil
100 g/⅔ cup plain, soft tofu
100 ml/½ cup oat or soy cream

900-g/2-lb. loaf pan, greased and lined with parchment paper

MAKES 1 LOAF CAKE

Preheat the oven to 180°C (350°F) Gas 4.

Steam the cubes of sweet potato for 10 minutes or until they are soft, but they should not fall apart when you prick them.

Sift together the flours, bicarbonate of soda/baking soda, baking powder, salt and sugar in a bowl and mix well.

Mix together the sparkling water and apple concentrate, then mix with the oil, tofu and cream until smooth.

Combine the dry and liquid ingredients and mix until smooth. Fold in the steamed cubes of potato, reserving a couple of pieces for decoration.

Pour the mixture into the prepared loaf pan and spread level with a spatula. Sprinkle the reserved sweet potatoes over the top and press them in lightly.

Bake the cake in the preheated oven for 25 minutes or until a skewer inserted in the centre comes out clean. Allow to cool in the pan for 10 minutes, then remove it, peel off the paper and allow to cool completely on a wire rack before serving.

The best way to keep the cake moist is wrapped in a clean kitchen towel.

Cook's tip: Instead of sparkling water and apple concentrate, you could use apple juice instead, but the sparkling water works well with bicarbonate of soda/baking soda and baking powder and makes this cake moist and spongy.

Chapter 3
Tea breads

Tea bread, Long Island style

Here's a tea bread with a difference — it contains boozy ingredients inspired by a Long Island Iced Tea cocktail! However, it goes very well with a traditional cup of tea, too.

2 teaspoons gin
2 teaspoons vodka
2 teaspoons rum
2 teaspoons tequila
2 teaspoons triple sec
150 g/¾ cup caster/granulated
    sugar
50 g/⅓ cup sultanas/golden raisins
50 g/⅓ cup glacé/candied
    cherries, roughly chopped
100 g/6½ tablespoons unsalted
    butter, softened, plus extra
    for greasing
1 teaspoon bicarbonate of soda/
    baking soda
1 egg, beaten
1 teaspoon baking powder
175 g/1⅓ cups plus 1 tablespoon
    plain/all-purpose flour

FOR DRIZZLING
1 tablespoon gin
1 tablespoon vodka
1 tablespoon rum
1 tablespoon tequila
1 tablespoon triple sec

*450-g/1-lb. loaf pan, greased and
    lined with parchment paper*

MAKES 1 LOAF CAKE

Preheat the oven to 180°C (350°F) Gas 4.

Pour all the alcohol for the tea bread into a large, heavy-based saucepan along with 70 ml/5 tablespoons water, and the sugar, sultanas/golden raisins, cherries, butter and bicarbonate of soda/baking soda. Set the pan over a medium heat and gradually bring to the boil, then keep it at a rolling boil for 10 minutes whilst gently stirring.

Remove the mixture from the heat and put to one side to cool for about 5 minutes, then add the beaten egg and the baking powder to the pan and stir in. Sift the flour over the mixture and give the mixture a good stir, then spoon into the prepared loaf pan.

Bake in the preheated oven for 40–50 minutes, until a skewer inserted into the centre comes out clean. Remove from the oven and prick the cake all over with a skewer.

Mix the 'drizzling' alcohol together in a small jug/pitcher and slowly pour over the cake. Allow the cake to cool for 5–10 minutes, then remove from the pan. Remove the paper and let it cool for a further 20–30 minutes on a wire rack.

Vegan rich tea bread

This is a recipe for a healthy combination of ingredients which are transformed into a very tasty vegan loaf that will make the whole family happy. The bonus is that many ingredients in this recipe can be replaced with any of the fruits, seeds and nuts that have been cluttering your kitchen cupboards for months!

60 g/½ cup dried plums
60 g/½ cup dates
40 g/⅓ cup dried cranberries
2 tablespoons dried goji berries
60 g/½ cup raisins
330 ml/1½ cups strong, hot tea
   (eg. rosehip and aniseed)
3 tablespoons brown rice or pure
   maple syrup
freshly squeezed juice and grated
   zest of 1 orange
65 g/⅓ cup sunflower oil, plus
   extra for greasing
200 g/1½ cups flour (eg.
   unbleached spelt flour plus
   unbleached plain/all-purpose
   flour)
1 teaspoon baking powder
1 teaspoon bicarbonate of soda/
   baking soda
¼ teaspoon salt
½ teaspoon ground cinnamon
¼ teaspoon ground nutmeg
¼ teaspoon ground ginger
110 g/⅔ cup chopped cashews
110 g/⅔ cup chopped walnuts
3 tablespoons chopped hazelnuts
   or pine nuts

*900-g/2-lb. loaf pan, oiled and
   lined with parchment paper*

MAKES 1 LOAF CAKE

Chop all the dried fruit into pieces roughly the same size as the raisins and place in a mixing bowl. Pour the strong, hot tea over the chopped fruit and set aside to steep for at least 30 minutes or longer.

Preheat the oven to 180°C (350°F) Gas 4.

Add the syrup, orange juice and zest and the oil to the bowl of soaked fruit and mix well.

In a separate bowl, mix together the flour, baking powder, bicarbonate of soda/baking soda, salt, cinnamon, nutmeg, ginger, cashews, walnuts and hazelnuts or pine nuts. Add them to the fruit mixture and mix again with a wooden spoon until thoroughly incorporated.

Spoon the cake mixture into the prepared loaf pan and spread level with a spatula. Bake in the preheated oven for 45–55 minutes or until a skewer inserted in the middle comes out clean. Allow to cool in the pan for 10 minutes, then remove and allow to cool completely on a wire rack.

Serve a slice of the cake with a cup of hot tea, of the same type used in the cake!

Mulled wine & cranberry tea bread

This loaf is studded with juicy fruit and nuts, perfect for eating during the colder months of the year. It is delicious sliced and eaten as it is or spread with unsalted butter.

a wine-mulling spice bag
200 ml/¾ cup light, fruity red wine
1 tablespoon runny honey
75 g/¾ cup ready-to-eat dried figs
50 g/3 balls crystallized stem ginger
75 g/⅔ cup whole blanched almonds
50 g/½ cup each dried cranberries and dried sour cherries (or use 100 g/¾ cup sultanas/golden raisins)
100 g/½ cup light muscovado or light brown soft sugar
2 large UK/extra large US eggs, lightly beaten
grated zest of 2 oranges
100 g/1 cup fresh cranberries
225 g/1¾ cups self-raising/self-rising flour
1 teaspoon ground cinnamon
½ teaspoon ground allspice

TOPPING
75 g/¾ cup dried cranberries (or dried sour cherries or sultanas/golden raisins)
2 tablespoons orange juice
4 tablespoons redcurrant jelly

900-g/2-lb. loaf pan, greased and lined with parchment paper

MAKES 1 LOAF CAKE

First make the mulled wine. Put the wine-mulling spice bag in a medium pan with the red wine and honey. Slowly bring to a simmer, stirring now and then. Leave over a very low heat for 5 minutes, then take the pan off the heat and set aside.

Roughly chop the figs, ginger and almonds and mix with the dried cranberries and cherries and the sugar in a mixing bowl. Remove the spice bag from the mulled wine, then pour the warm wine over the dried fruit and leave to soak for 30 minutes.

Preheat the oven to 160°C (325°F) Gas 3.

Stir the beaten eggs, orange zest and the fresh cranberries into the soaked dried fruit. Next, sift in the flour, cinnamon and allspice. Mix together until thoroughly combined.

Spoon the mixture into the prepared loaf pan. Bake in the preheated oven for 55 minutes, by which time the loaf will have risen and slightly shrunk from the sides of the pan. Leave to cool in the pan, then tip the loaf out and peel off the paper.

To make the topping, gently heat the cranberries, orange juice and redcurrant jelly in a small pan over a low heat, stirring until the jelly has dissolved.

Brush the top of the loaf with some of the sticky juices from the topping, then spoon the cranberries along the centre of the loaf. Leave to cool before serving.

Fruit bread

This traditional favourite is so simple to make and makes a delicious teatime treat that actually tastes better a day or two after baking. Serve it thickly spread with butter and accompanied by a cup of your favourite tea. It is equally delicious toasted.

35 g/2½ tablespoons salted butter, softened
65 g/⅓ cup packed dark brown sugar
1 egg
1 tablespoon black treacle/dark molasses
165 g/1⅓ cups self-raising/self-rising flour
a pinch of salt
¼ teaspoon mixed spice/apple pie spice
¼ teaspoon ground cinnamon
65 g/½ cup sultanas/golden raisins
25 g/3 tablespoons chopped pecans

450-g/1-lb. loaf pan, lined with parchment paper

MAKES 1 LOAF CAKE

Preheat the oven to 170°C (325°F) Gas 3.

In a large bowl, cream the butter and sugar together until paler and fluffy. Add the egg and beat in.

In a separate bowl, combine 90 ml/6 tablespoons warm water and the treacle/molasses, then add to the creamed butter and stir to mix. Sift together the flour, salt and spices. Add to the bowl, followed by the sultanas/golden raisins and pecans, and beat to a smooth mixture.

Spoon the mixture into the prepared loaf pan and bake in the preheated oven for 40–45 minutes or until the top springs back from light finger pressure or a skewer inserted into the middle of the loaf comes out clean.

The bread is best stored overnight and then served spread with butter. It will keep for up to 5 days in an airtight container.

Almond flour tea loaf with fresh berries

If you are new to baking with almond flour, you may be surprised to learn that it doesn't require any starches or binding agents to make delicious baked goods. This loaf makes a great breakfast treat.

165 g/1½ cup almond flour
50 g/½ cup milled flaxseeds
1½ teaspoons baking powder
100 g/heaping 1 cup coconut
   sugar
125 g/½ cup melted coconut oil
1 teaspoon vanilla extract
4 eggs (see Note)

TO SERVE
a handful of fresh berries
a dollop of clotted/thick cream

*450-g/1-lb. loaf pan, lined with
   parchment paper*

MAKES 1 LOAF CAKE

Preheat the oven to 180°C (350°F) Gas 4.

Sift the almond flour into a large mixing bowl. Add in the other dry ingredients, then the melted oil and vanilla and mix together. Then add the eggs, and whisk using a hand-held electric whisk on high speed for 4 minutes until the batter becomes light and increases in volume. Pour into the prepared loaf pan.

Bake in the preheated oven for 40 minutes or until a skewer inserted into the centre comes out clean.

Garnish with fresh seasonal berries and serve with a dollop of cream on the side.

Note: If you prefer not to use eggs, you could use egg replacer or make a flax-egg mix by combining 2 tablespoons of ground flaxseed with 6 tablespoons of water.

Chocolate, cherry & macadamia tea breads

There's something about the combination of dark chocolate and bitter cherries that is beguiling. These moist little teabreads are studded with those succulent cherries in syrup often found spooned over ice cream in Italian ice cream parlours. Creamy macadamia nuts add an extra layer of luxury to these already decadent teabreads.

300 g/2⅓ cups plain/all-purpose flour
50 g/6 tablespoons unsweetened cocoa powder
3 teaspoons baking powder
½ teaspoon bicarbonate of soda/baking soda
½ teaspoon salt
350 ml/1⅓ cups milk
100 g/⅔ cup amarena cherries, plus 100 ml/6 tablespoons of their syrup
75 g/⅓ cup light brown soft sugar
50 g/3 tablespoons unsalted butter, softened, plus extra for greasing
100 g/3½ oz. dark/bittersweet chocolate, broken into pieces
150 g/1 cup macadamia nuts, roughly chopped, plus extra to scatter

8 mini loaf pans, greased and base-lined with parchment paper

MAKES 8

Preheat the oven to 150°C (300°F) Gas 2.

Sift the flour, cocoa, baking powder, bicarbonate of soda/baking soda and salt together in a large bowl.

Heat the milk, amarena cherry syrup, sugar, butter and chocolate together in a medium pan until melted and smooth. Stir this into the flour mixture as quickly as possible until just combined. Stir in the cherries and macadamia nuts, then spoon into the prepared pans and smooth the surface. Scatter with extra macadamia nuts.

Bake in the preheated oven for about 30 minutes or until firm and a skewer inserted into the centre comes out clean. Remove from the oven and leave to cool in the pans for 10 minutes, then turn out onto a wire rack and leave to cool completely.

Store in an airtight container for 1 day to mature before serving.

Note: If you don't have any mini loaf pans, you can use two 450-g/1-lb. loaf pans and bake for 1 hour.

Bara brith

*Bara brith is literally translated from the Welsh as 'speckled bread',
though no yeast is required. This tasty, traditional tea bread is best
served warmed or toasted and spread with plenty of butter.*

2 tea bags
130 ml/½ cup boiling water
100 g/½ cup packed dark brown
  sugar
75 g/½ cup Zante currants
75 g/½ cup sultanas/golden raisins
180 g/1½ cups self-raising/
  self-rising flour
½ teaspoon mixed spice/apple
  pie spice
½ teaspoon ground cinnamon
¼ teaspoon ground ginger
1 egg

*450-g/1-lb. loaf pan, lined with
  parchment paper*

MAKES 1 LOAF CAKE

Start the bara brith the day before you want to serve it. Put the tea bags
and boiling water into a jug/pitcher and allow to stand for 15 minutes
before removing the tea bags.

Put the sugar, currants and sultanas/golden raisins into a large bowl,
add the tea and stir together. Cover with a kitchen towel and allow to
stand and infuse overnight.

The next day, preheat the oven to 170°C (325°F) Gas 3.

Add the flour, spices and egg to the fruit and tea mixture and mix
until well combined.

Spoon the mixture into the prepared pan and bake in the preheated
oven for 1 hour. Remove from the oven, cover the loaf with foil and bake
for a further 15 minutes or until a skewer inserted into the middle of the
loaf comes out clean. Allow to cool on a wire rack. Serve thickly spread
with butter.

This loaf will keep for 4–5 days in an airtight container.

Sticky marzipan & cherry loaf

Studded with sweet glacé cherries and with a surprise layer of sticky marzipan running through the centre, this simple loaf cake will hit the spot at teatime.

175 g/1½ sticks butter, at room temperature, plus extra for greasing
175 g/¾ cup caster/granulated sugar
3 eggs
175 g/1 cup self-raising/self-rising flour
85 g/scant 1 cup ground almonds
175 g/6 oz. glacé cherries, halved
75 g/2¾ oz. chilled marzipan, finely grated
icing/confectioner's sugar, for dusting

900-g/2-lb loaf pan, greased and lined with parchment paper

MAKES 1 LOAF CAKE

Preheat the oven to 180°C (350°F) Gas 4.

Put the butter and sugar in a large mixing bowl and beat until pale and creamy. Beat in the eggs one at a time. Sift the flour onto the mixture and then fold in. Stir in the cherries until evenly distributed in the mixture.

Spoon half the mixture into the prepared loaf pan and level the surface. Sprinkle with the grated marzipan. Top with the remaining mixture and smooth the surface.

Bake in the preheated oven for about 45 minutes, then remove the cake from the oven and cover the top with foil. Return it to the oven and bake for a further 25 minutes, until risen and golden and a skewer inserted in the centre of the cake comes out clean.

Leave to cool in the pan for about 10 minutes, then lift out on to a wire rack to cool. Serve the cake dusted with sugar and slightly warm or at room temperature.

Sticky gingerbread loaf

Sticky, sweet, spicy ginger cake, served slathered in butter and still warm from the oven, served on an autumnal afternoon with a pot of Assam tea, is about as good as afternoon tea gets.

100 g/7 tablespoons butter, plus extra for greasing
100 g/5 tablespoons golden/light corn syrup
100 g/5 tablespoons black treacle/molasses
100 g/½ cup soft dark brown sugar
200 g/1½ cups self-raising/self-rising flour
2 tablespoons five-spice powder
2 teaspoons ground ginger
100 g/3½ oz. stem ginger, finely chopped
1 egg
250 ml/1 cup milk

900-g/2-lb. loaf pan, greased and lined with parchment paper

MAKES 1 LOAF CAKE

Preheat the oven to 140°C (280°F) Gas 1.

In a heavy-based saucepan, melt the butter, golden/light corn syrup, black treacle/molasses and brown sugar over a low heat, stirring to combine.

In a mixing bowl, combine the flour, five-spice powder and ground ginger and stir to combine. Add the stem ginger and mix, ensuring the ginger pieces are coated with the flour mixture and not clumped together.

Whisk the egg and milk together.

Add the melted ingredients to the flour mixture in the mixing bowl and fold together to combine. Add the whisked milk and egg mixture whilst continuing to fold together, until you have a smooth, even batter.

Pour the batter into the prepared loaf pan and bake in the preheated oven for 60–70 minutes, until a skewer poked into the centre comes out clean. Remove from the oven and leave the cake to cool for 20 minutes before removing from the pan.

Serve in generous slices with plenty of butter.

Apricot & nut loaf

This fat-free, fruit and nut loaf is the perfect accompaniment to a pot of Earl Grey tea. The apricot topping adds an extra delicious layer, as well as looking so pretty.

60 g/½ cup wholemeal/
   whole-wheat flour
30 g/3 tablespoons ground
   almonds
160 g/¾ cup packed dark brown
   sugar
140 g/1 cup sultanas/golden
   raisins
120 g/1 cup chopped dried
   apricots
75 g/½ cup chopped mixed nuts
2 eggs, lightly beaten

TOPPING
10 whole dried apricots
50 g/3 tablespoons apricot jam/
   preserves

*450-g/1-lb. loaf pan, lined with
   parchment paper*

MAKES 1 LOAF CAKE

Preheat the oven to 150°C (300°F) Gas 2.

Put the flour, ground almonds, sugar, sultanas/golden raisins, chopped apricots and nuts in a large bowl and mix together. Add the beaten eggs and stir well.

Spoon the mixture into the prepared loaf pan, smooth level and top with the whole dried apricots.

Bake in the preheated oven for 1 hour or until a skewer inserted into centre comes out clean. Remove from the oven and allow to cool in the pan.

Boil the apricot jam in a small saucepan and carefully pour over the top of the loaf to glaze it. When completely cool, remove the loaf from the pan. Serve in thin slices.

The loaf will keep for up to 14 days wrapped in clingfilm/plastic wrap and sealed in an airtight container.

Variation: To make a Date & Nut Loaf, simply replace the dried apricots in both the cake and the topping with the same quantity of pitted dates.

Gluten-free 'malt' loaf

This is not technically a malt loaf, as traditional malt extract is made from barley. Instead, this gluten-free recipe uses brown teff flour and molasses to impart a similar flavour. The loaf can be served as soon as it's cool enough, but ideally, wrap and keep for 24–48 hours before slicing, to allow the stickiness to intensify.

150 g/1 cup chopped dried dates
220 ml/1 scant cup hot black tea, made with 2 tea bags
100 ml/6½ tablespoons black treacle/molasses
50 g/¼ cup soft light brown sugar
115 g/¾ cup brown teff flour
115 g/¾ cup plain/all-purpose gluten-free flour
1 teaspoon baking powder
½ teaspoon xanthan gum
¼ teaspoon salt
15 g/1 tablespoon sunflower oil
2 eggs
175 g/1 generous cup sultanas/golden raisins
butter, softened, to serve (optional)

900-g/2-lb. loaf pan, greased and lined with parchment paper

MAKES 1 LOAF CAKE

Preheat the oven to 170°C (325°F) Gas 3.

Put the dates and tea into a saucepan and bring to a simmer over a gentle heat for 5 minutes until the dates have softened. Remove from the heat and, using a stick/immersion blender, blitz for 30–60 seconds until just about smooth. If you don't have a stick blender, allow the dates to simmer for a further 5–10 minutes, remove from the heat and continue without blending them.

Stir in the treacle/molasses and brown sugar until well combined, then add the flours, baking powder, xanthan gum, salt, oil and eggs. Beat with a wooden spoon until smooth – the batter will be quite thick.

Stir in the sultanas/golden raisins, then transfer the mixture to the prepared loaf pan. Level the top and bake in the preheated oven for 1 hour, checking after 50 minutes that the top of the loaf isn't browning too much. Cover with foil if so.

Take the loaf out of the oven once it feels firm and allow to cool in the pan. Brush the top of the cake with extra treacle/molasses while still warm.

Remove the loaf from the pan when cool and, ideally, wrap in parchment paper and foil, allowing it to rest for a day or two before eating.

Note: Malt loaf can be sliced and lightly toasted to serve warm, if desired, or to bring it back to life if it has become a little stale.

Pain d'épices

This is a delicious French gingerbread cake. Make it a couple of days before you want to eat it so that the flavours of all the spices have time to mellow with the honey. Serve it in slices on its own or with a lick of butter.

225 g/1¾ cups plain/all-purpose flour
2 teaspoons baking powder
1 teaspoon ground cinnamon
3 teaspoons ground ginger
¼ teaspoon ground allspice
¼ teaspoon ground cloves
¼ teaspoon salt
150 g/10 tablespoons unsalted butter, softened, plus extra for greasing
75 g/⅓ cup light brown soft sugar
125 ml/½ cup clear honey
2 eggs, lightly beaten
3–4 tablespoons milk

900-g/2-lb. loaf pan, greased and lined with parchment paper

MAKES 1 LOAF CAKE

Preheat the oven to 180°C (350°F) Gas 4.

Sift the flour, baking powder, cinnamon, ginger, allspice, cloves and salt together into a mixing bowl and set aside.

Put the butter and sugar in the bowl of a stand mixer (or use a large mixing bowl and a hand-held electric whisk) and cream them until pale and light.

Add the honey and mix again. Gradually add the beaten eggs, mixing well between each addition and scraping down the bowl with a rubber spatula from time to time.

Add the sifted dry ingredients and the milk and mix again until smooth. Spoon into the prepared loaf pan and spread evenly with a knife.

Bake in the preheated oven for about 1 hour, or until well risen and a skewer inserted into the middle comes out clean. You may need to cover the cake loosely with a sheet of foil if it is browning too quickly.

Leave it to cool in the pan for 5 minutes before tipping out onto a wire rack to cool completely.

Chapter 4
Muffins & small cakes

Blueberry muffins

The official state muffin of Minnesota, the blueberry muffin has become as synonymous with American breakfasts as the croissant is with France. These sweet, yeast-free, quick bread treats, studded with juicy blueberries, are so easy to make and are delicious enough to be enjoyed at any time of the day.

250 ml/1 cup buttermilk
100 g/6½ tablespoons unsalted butter, melted and cooled slightly
1 large UK/extra large US egg, beaten
250 g/2 cups plain/all-purpose flour
1 teaspoon baking powder
1 teaspoon bicarbonate of soda/baking soda
200 g/1 cup caster/granulated sugar
a pinch of salt
200 g/1⅓ cups fresh blueberries

12-hole muffin pan, lined with paper cases

MAKES 12

Whisk together the buttermilk, melted butter and egg in a large glass measuring jug/cup.

Sift together the flour, baking powder and bicarbonate of soda/baking soda in a large mixing bowl and add the sugar and salt. Pour the wet ingredients into the dry and use a fork to gently combine. Leave the batter to rest for at least 1 hour or in the fridge overnight.

Preheat the oven to 200°C (400°F) Gas 6.

Fold the blueberries into the batter, then divide the mixture among the paper cases, trying to make sure the blueberries are fairly evenly distributed.

Bake in the preheated oven for 20–25 minutes, or until a skewer inserted into the centre of a muffin comes out clean. Remove from the oven and transfer to a wire rack. Allow to cool slightly before tucking in.

Chocolate & pecan muffins

Surely there will always be a place for muffins in every baker's repertoire of recipes. Dark, glossy and inviting, this moist and nutty chocolate version is quick to make and freezes well, so you need never be short of the kind of cake that gave rise to the term 'comfort food'.

260 g/2 cups plain/all-purpose
   flour
1 tablespoon baking powder
a pinch of salt
60 g/½ cup unsweetened cocoa
   powder
100 g/⅔ cup roughly chopped
   pecans
180 g/scant cup caster/granulated
   sugar
150 g/1 cup dark/bittersweet
   chocolate chips
180 ml/¾ cup corn oil
2 eggs
210 ml/¾ cup plus 2 tablespoons
   milk
1 teaspoon vanilla extract

*12-hole muffin pan, lined with
   paper cases*

MAKES 12

Preheat the oven to 190°C (375°F) Gas 5.

Put the flour, baking powder, salt, cocoa powder, pecans, sugar and chocolate chips in a large bowl. In a separate bowl, whisk together the corn oil, eggs, milk and vanilla extract, then pour onto the dry ingredients. Beat all the ingredients together until just smooth.

Spoon the mixture into the paper cases, filling them about three-quarters full. Bake in the preheated oven for 25–30 minutes or until well risen and a skewer inserted into the centre of a muffin comes out clean. Remove from the oven, transfer to a wire rack and allow to cool slightly.

The muffins are best served slightly warm. They can be frozen for up to 2 months.

Crunchy-topped raspberry & banana muffins

Delicious warm or cold, for breakfast or to accompany a cup of tea, these muffins are also ideal for packed lunches and they freeze well. Another time, use blueberries instead of the raspberries to ring the changes.

150 g/1¼ sticks butter
2 very ripe bananas
150 ml/⅔ cup milk
150 g/¾ cup caster/granulated
    sugar
3 large UK/extra large US eggs
300 g/2¼ cups self-raising/
    self-rising flour
1 slightly rounded teaspoon baking
    powder
150 g/1 cup raspberries
3–4 tablespoons demerara/
    turbinado sugar
2 tablespoons sunflower seeds

*12-hole muffin pan, lined with
paper cases*

MAKES 12

Preheat the oven to 200°C (400°F) Gas 6.

Melt the butter in a small pan and leave to cool slightly. Peel and mash the bananas.

In a large mixing bowl and using a balloon whisk, whisk together the milk, caster/granulated sugar, eggs and melted butter. Sift in the flour and baking powder and add the raspberries and banana. Using a large metal spoon, fold everything together until combined, but don't over-mix.

Divide the mixture between the muffin cases. Sprinkle the top of each muffin with a little demerara/turbinado sugar and the sunflower seeds. Bake in the preheated oven for 30–35 minutes, or until risen and golden and a skewer inserted into the centre of a muffin comes out clean. Leave to cool on a wire rack.

Blueberry muffins with lemon & white chocolate

Ripe blueberries make the perfect partner for tangy lemon and creamy white chocolate. These muffins are at their most delicious when made with blueberries in season, but you can still bake them at any time of year using frozen fruit.

180 g/1½ sticks unsalted butter
150 ml/⅔ cup whole/full-fat milk
350 g/2⅔ cups self-raising/
   self-rising flour
150 g/¾ cup golden caster/
   granulated sugar
1 teaspoon baking powder
2 tablespoons freshly squeezed
   lemon juice
2 eggs, beaten
finely grated zest of 1 lemon
1 teaspoon vanilla extract
100 g/⅔ cup white chocolate,
   roughly chopped
150 g/1¼ cups blueberries
light muscovado sugar, to sprinkle

*12-hole muffin pan, lined with
   paper cases*

MAKES 12

Preheat the oven to 180°C (350°F) Gas 4.

Put the butter and milk in a saucepan and heat gently until the butter melts. Take off the heat and leave to cool for 5 minutes.

Put the flour, caster/granulated sugar and baking powder into a large bowl and make a well in the centre.

Add the lemon juice to the milk and butter mixture and then add the wet mixture to the dry ingredients and stir together. Don't overmix the batter as this will make the muffins tough.

Stir in the eggs, then add the lemon zest, vanilla, chocolate and 100 g/1 cup of the blueberries, reserving the remainder to top the muffins.

Fill each muffin case two-thirds of the way up (to give them room to rise) and then squash the extra blueberries into the top of each muffin and sprinkle with the muscovado sugar. Bake in the preheated oven for about 20–25 minutes, until risen, golden brown on top and a skewer inserted into the centre of a muffin comes out clean.

Allow the muffins to cool in the pan for a few minutes before transferring them to a wire rack to cool completely.

The muffins will keep stored in an airtight container for 3–4 days, but do warm them before eating.

Double chocolate chip muffins

Light, fluffy and studded with chocolate chips, these muffins are such a cinch to make and even easier to eat.

250 ml/1 cup buttermilk
100 g/6½ tablespoons butter
1 large egg, beaten
200 g/1⅔ cups plain/all-purpose flour
50 g/scant ½ cup cocoa powder
1 teaspoon baking powder
1 teaspoon bicarbonate of soda/baking soda
200 g/1 cup caster/granulated sugar
a pinch of salt
150 g/¾ cup dark/bittersweet or milk/semi-sweet chocolate chips (or a mixture of the two)

12-hole muffin pan, lined with paper cases

MAKES 12

Preheat the oven to 190°C (375°F) Gas 5.

Melt the butter in a small pan and leave to cool slightly. Whisk together the buttermilk, melted butter and egg in a large jug/pitcher.

Sift together the flour, cocoa, baking powder and bicarbonate of soda/baking soda in a separate large mixing bowl and add the sugar and salt.

Pour the dry ingredients into the wet and use a fork to gently combine. Do not overmix the batter. Fold in 100 g/⅔ cup of the chocolate chips.

Pour the batter into the paper cases, sprinkle over the remaining chocolate chips and bake in the preheated oven for 20–25 minutes, or until a skewer inserted into the centre of a muffin comes out clean.

Transfer the muffins onto a wire rack to cool slightly before tucking in.

Chocolate & banana muffins

100 g/¾ cup sultanas/golden raisins

75 ml/5 tablespoons freshly squeezed orange juice

250 g/1¾ cups plus 2 tablespoons plain/all-purpose flour

1 teaspoon bicarbonate of soda/ baking soda

1 teaspoon baking powder

100 g/1 cup chopped dates

75 g/½ cup dark/bittersweet chocolate, chopped

1 teaspoon ground cinnamon

1 egg, beaten

80 g/6½ tablespoons light muscovado sugar, plus extra to sprinkle

80 g/6 tablespoons unsalted butter, melted

2 large ripe bananas, mashed

175 ml/¾ cup whole/full-fat milk

12-hole muffin pan, lined with paper cases

MAKES 12

Banana and chocolate is a favourite flavour combination with kids of all ages and works brilliantly in this moist muffin, which is packed full of not just bananas but also dates, orange-infused sultanas/golden raisins, a hint of cinnamon and plenty of chunks of dark chocolate to keep the chocoholics happy. They are at their most delicious served warm, and can be frozen for up to 2 weeks. To serve, simply let defrost and warm in a low oven.

Preheat the oven to 180°C (350°F) Gas 4.

Put the sultanas/golden raisins in a small saucepan and add the orange juice. Bring to the boil, then take off the heat and set aside to allow the sultanas to plump up.

Put the flour, bicarbonate of soda/baking soda, baking powder, three-quarters of the dates, the chocolate and cinnamon in a separate bowl and make a well in the centre.

Beat the egg and muscovado sugar together, then add the melted butter, bananas, milk and orange juice-soaked sultanas/golden raisins.

Add the egg mixture to the dry ingredients and stir together. Don't overmix the batter as this will make the muffins tough. The mixture will be quite runny but that's nothing to worry about.

Fill each muffin case two-thirds of the way up (to give them room to rise). Scatter the remaining chopped dates on top of each muffin and sprinkle with the brown sugar. Bake in the preheated oven for about 20–25 minutes, until golden brown and a skewer inserted in the centre of a muffin comes out clean.

Allow the muffins to cool in the pan for a few minutes before transferring to a wire rack to cool completely.

The muffins will keep stored in an airtight container for 3–4 days, or can be frozen for up to 2 weeks. Do warm them in a low oven before eating.

Toffee pear muffins

The toffee in these muffins is dulce de leche: thick, luscious caramel, sold in cans or jars. It also makes a delicious sauce to serve with sautéed pears, apples or bananas, for a quick dessert, if you have some left over.

150 g/1¼ sticks butter

150 ml/⅔ cup milk

3 large UK/extra large US eggs

6 tablespoons dulce de leche

100 g/½ cup light brown soft sugar, plus extra for sprinkling

300 g/2⅓ cups self-raising/self-rising flour

1 generous teaspoon baking powder

2 rounded teaspoons mixed spice/apple pie spice

2 large, ripe but firm pears, cored, peeled and chopped into small pieces

1 rounded tablespoon porridge/rolled oats

12-hole muffin pan, lined with paper cases

MAKES 12

Preheat the oven to 200°C (400°F) Gas 6.

Melt the butter in a small pan and leave to cool slightly.

In a large mixing bowl and using a balloon whisk, whisk together the milk, eggs, 2 tablespoons of the dulce de leche, the sugar and the melted butter.

Sift in the flour, baking powder and mixed spice and whisk together. Scatter the chopped pear over the top and, using a large metal spoon, gently fold it in until just combined.

Divide the mixture (which will be quite sloppy) between the muffin cases. Sprinkle each muffin with a little extra sugar and a few porridge oats. Bake the muffins in the preheated oven for 30–35 minutes, or until risen and lightly golden.

Leave the muffins to cool for 10 minutes or so, then, using a small, sharp knife, cut a small cross in the top of each muffin and spoon ½ teaspoon of dulce de leche into each one. Leave it to settle, then add another ½ teaspoon to sit on top. Eat while still warm.

Cream cheese coffee cake muffins

American coffee cake is traditionally a soft, cinnamon-spiced cake with a crunchy streusel topping that is served with a cup of coffee, but it doesn't actually have any coffee in it. The addition of cream cheese makes these muffins beautifully light.

250 g/2 cups self-raising/
    self-rising flour
225 g/1 cup plus 2 tablespoons
    caster/granulated sugar
a pinch of salt
1 teaspoon ground cinnamon
150 g/1 stick plus 2 tablespoons
    unsalted butter, at room
    temperature
2 UK large/US extra-large eggs
150 g/¾ cup full-fat cream
    cheese, at room temperature
100 g/½ cup light brown sugar

*12-hole muffin pan, lined with
    large paper cases*

MAKES 12

Preheat the oven to 180°C (350°F) Gas 4.

In a large bowl, using your hands, carefully combine the flour, caster/granulated sugar, salt, cinnamon and butter until you have a sandy texture. Take out 120 g/4 oz. of this mixture and set it aside in a small bowl (this will form part of the crumb topping later).

Add the eggs and cream cheese into the large bowl, and beat just until you have a smooth cake batter.

Into the small bowl, add the light brown sugar and carefully mix, but don't worry if there are still lumps – lumps are good for a crumb topping!

Using an ice-cream scoop, fill the paper cases with the cake batter. Sprinkle the crumb topping over each muffin, making sure the entire surface is covered, and lightly push the topping into the muffin.

Bake in the preheated oven for about 20 minutes until each muffin is golden brown and a skewer inserted into the centre comes out clean. (Some of the topping will fall off during baking, but this is normal.)

Once baked, remove from the oven and allow them to cool in the pan for about 5 minutes, before transferring to a wire rack.

These muffins are delicious served hot, straight from the oven, but can be stored for up to 3 days in an airtight container.

Gluten-free lemon & amaretto loaf cakes

Lemon and almond are a match made in heaven. The drizzle ensures that these little loaf cakes stay nice and moist and the drizzle and almond topping finish them off to perfection.

115 g/1 stick butter, softened
115g/½ cup plus 1 tablespoon caster/granulated sugar
2 large eggs
60 g/ ½ cup self-raising/self-rising gluten-free flour OR 60 g/½ cup plain/all-purpose gluten-free baking flour plus ½ teaspoon baking powder and ⅛ teaspoon xanthan gum
60 g/½ cup ground almonds
80 ml/⅓ cup plain yogurt
grated zest of 2 lemons

DRIZZLE
60 ml/¼ cup amaretto
1 tablespoon caster/superfine sugar
freshly squeezed juice of 2 lemons

TOPPING
160 g/1 cup icing/confectioner's sugar
freshly squeezed juice of 2 lemons
flaked/slivered almonds

6 mini loaf pans, greased and lined with parchment paper

MAKES 6

Preheat the oven to 180°C (350°F) Gas 4.

Put the butter and sugar in a mixing bowl and whisk until light and creamy. Add the eggs and whisk again. Fold in the flour, ground almonds, yogurt and lemon zest using a spatula. Put a large spoonful of cake batter into each prepared loaf pan.

Bake in the preheated oven for about 20–25 minutes, until the cakes are firm to the touch and golden brown and a skewer inserted into the centre comes out clean.

To make the drizzle, put the amaretto, sugar and lemon juice in a small saucepan and heat until the sugar has dissolved. Pour over the warm cakes and leave to cool in the pans.

To make the topping, mix the icing/confectioner's sugar and lemon juice together, adding a little extra water if the icing is too stiff. Remove the cakes from the pans, spoon a little icing over the top of each cake and sprinkle with almonds.

The cakes will keep for up to 2 days in an airtight container.

Gluten-free lemon polenta cakes

These delicious flourless citrussy treats are packed with zingy lemon zest and syrup, making them beautifully moist.

200 g/1 stick plus 6 tablespoons butter, plus extra for greasing
230 g/1 cup plus 2½ tablespoons golden caster/raw cane sugar
3 eggs
200 g/1⅓ cups ground almonds
100 g/¾ cup polenta/cornmeal
1 teaspoon baking powder
3 lemons

LEMON ICING
1 tablespoon freshly squeezed lemon juice
250 g/2 cups icing/confectioner's sugar

6 x 170-ml/6-oz. pudding moulds, greased and base-lined with a small circle of parchment paper

MAKES 6

Preheat the oven to 170°C (325°F) Gas 3.

Beat the butter and 200 g/1 cup of the sugar together in a large mixing bowl, until light and fluffy. Add the eggs, one at a time, beating well after each addition. Add small amounts of ground almonds if the mixture begins to curdle. Add in the remaining ground almonds and beat well. Stir in the polenta/cornmeal and baking powder. Add the grated zest and freshly squeezed juice of ½ a lemon and stir again.

Divide the batter evenly between the prepared pudding moulds and put them on a baking sheet. Bake in the preheated oven for 20 minutes or until a skewer inserted into a cake comes out clean.

Meanwhile, make a lemon syrup. Put the zest and juice of the remaining lemons (save a tablespoon of juice for the icing) in a saucepan set over a gentle heat, with the remaining sugar. Stir to combine and heat until the sugar has dissolved completely.

Remove the cakes from the oven and prick all over with a skewer. Pour the lemon syrup over each cake and let it soak through – about 1 tablespoon per cake. Let cool in the moulds for 15 minutes before turning the cakes out to cool completely.

To make the lemon icing, add just enough lemon juice to the icing/confectioners' sugar for a thick but slightly runny consistency. When ready to serve, spoon the lemon icing on top of the cakes and let it drip down their sides.

Beetroot, cherry & chocolate cakes

The flavour of beetroot/beets works so well with chocolate, and also gives these cakes slightly squidgy centres. If you wish, dust the tops with cocoa powder. The cakes also freeze well, that's if you don't eat them all on the day of baking!

75 g/2¾ oz. dark/bittersweet chocolate (about 50% cocoa solids)

50 g/½ cup dried sour cherries (or dried cranberries)

175 g /1⅓ cups self-raising/ self-rising flour

40 g/scant ½ cup cocoa powder

175 g/¾ cup plus 2 tablespoons light muscovado or light brown soft sugar

250 ml/1 cup groundnut or vegetable oil

3 large UK/extra large US eggs

a pinch of salt

150 g/5½ oz. cooked, peeled beetroot/beets

9-hole mini loaf pan (each hole 5.5 x 8 cm/2¼ x 3¼ inches and 2.5 cm/1 inch deep), lined with paper cases

MAKES 9

Preheat the oven to 180°C (350°F) Gas 4.

Break the chocolate into pieces and melt it in a heatproof bowl set over a pan of barely simmering water. Leave to cool slightly.

Roughly chop the sour cherries.

Sift the flour into the bowl of a stand mixer (or use a large mixing bowl and a hand-held electric whisk). Add the cocoa, sugar, oil, eggs, salt and the melted chocolate, and whisk until combined. Using the coarse side of a grater, grate the beetroot/beets into the mixture and sprinkle in the chopped sour cherries. Using a large metal spoon, fold everything together gently. Divide the mixture between the loaf cases.

Bake in the preheated oven for 20–25 minutes, or until well risen and a skewer inserted into the centre comes out clean. Leave the cakes to cool completely in the pan.

Cook's tip: If you prefer, you can bake the cakes in muffin cases instead of mini-loaf cases – they will take 25–30 minutes in the oven, and make 9 muffins.

200 g/1 cup light muscovado/
brown sugar
100 ml/⅓ cup plus 1 tablespoon
sunflower oil
3 large eggs
1 teaspoon vanilla paste
225 g/1 lb. peeled and cooked
beetroot/beets (approx.
2–3 beetroot/beets), blended
to a purée
200 g/6½ oz. dark/bittersweet
chocolate (60–70% cocoa
solids), melted and cooled
50 g/⅓ cup ground almonds
115 g/1 scant cup self-raising/
self-rising flour
½ teaspoon bicarbonate of soda/
baking soda
½ teaspoon baking powder
a pinch of salt

ICING
50 g/1½ oz. dark/bittersweet
chocolate (60–70% cocoa
solids), chopped
25 g/2 tablespoons butter
40 ml/2½ tablespoons sweetened
condensed milk
2 tablespoons golden/light corn
syrup

CHOCOLATE & COURGETTE
LOAF VARIATION
250 g/8 oz. courgettes/ zucchini,
coarsely grated
1 teaspoon ground cinnamon
(optional)

*12 mini loaf pans (each 8 x 4 cm/
3¼ x 1¾ inches), greased and
set on a baking sheet (or a
900-g/2-lb. loaf pan, greased
– see Cook's tip)*

MAKES 12

Chocolate & beetroot mini loaf cakes

Beets add a mild note of earthiness that makes these cakes incredibly moist. The courgettes/zucchini also add moisture, while a hint of spice enlivens the chocolate.

Preheat the oven to 180°C (350°F) Gas 4.

Put the sugar, oil, eggs and vanilla in a large mixing bowl and whisk until frothy. Add the puréed beetroot/beets, melted chocolate and ground almonds and whisk again until fully mixed. Sift the flour, bicarbonate of soda/baking soda and baking powder, and add the salt before folding in. Pour the batter into the mini loaf pans

Bake in the preheated oven for 20–25 minutes, or until a skewer inserted into the centre comes out clean. Transfer the loaves, still in their pans, to a wire rack to cool completely.

To make the icing, simply melt and stir all the ingredients together in a heatproof bowl placed over a pan of barely simmering water until smooth and glossy. Drizzle the icing over the top of the cakes and enjoy.

Variation: You can substitute courgettes/zucchini for the beetroots/beets in these mini vegetable loaf cakes – simply add where you would the beetroots/beets as above along with the ground cinnamon to balance the flavours.

Cook's tip: If using a 900-g/2-lb. loaf pan, adjust the baking time to 45–60 minutes, or until a skewer inserted into the centre comes out clean.

Chapter 5
Other easy bakes

Rock cakes

These tasty little cakes are so named because of their resemblance to rocks, not because they are rock hard! A traditional British teatime treat, rock cakes are child's play to make. In fact, they require such minimal labour, you can delegate them to children to rustle up while you put your feet up.

220 g/1¾ cups self-raising/
  self-rising flour
1 teaspoon baking powder
75 g/⅓ cup caster/granulated
  sugar
a pinch of salt
110 g/7 tablespoons cold butter,
  cut into cubes
1 egg
1 tablespoon whole/full-fat milk
50 g/⅓ cup dried (Zante) currants
50 g/⅓ cup sultanas/golden raisins
50 g/⅓ cup (dark) raisins

*2 baking sheets, lined with
  parchment paper*

MAKES 12

Preheat the oven to 180°C (350°F) Gas 4.

Sift the flour and baking powder into a large mixing bowl and stir in the sugar and salt. Rub the butter into the flour mixture with the tips of your fingers, until the mixture resembles fine breadcrumbs.

Make a well in the centre of the bowl and crack in the egg and then add the milk. Use a fork to whisk the egg and milk together and gradually mix the dry ingredients into the wet. Once combined, the mixture should be stiff but not dry. You can add a little extra milk at this stage if you need to. Add the dried fruit and mix well.

Dollop rounded teaspoons of the mixture on to the prepared baking sheets, with a space in between to allow for spreading.

Bake in the preheated oven for 15–20 minutes, or until firm and slightly golden on top. Transfer the rock cakes to a wire rack to cool.

Buttermilk scones

No afternoon tea is complete without a tray of still-warm, crumbly scones with lashings of clotted cream and (preferably) homemade strawberry jam. Scones are one of the quickest and easiest teatime treats to make, however they do require a light touch as over-working the dough will result in tough, dry scones. The less you handle the dough, the better the scones will be. There's only one real dilemma here – whether to put the cream or the jam on first.

450 g/3½ cups plain/all-purpose flour, plus extra for dusting
2 teaspoons baking powder
a pinch of salt
100 g/7 tablespoons butter, chilled and diced
75 g/⅓ cup caster/granulated sugar
250 ml/1 cup buttermilk
1 egg white, lightly beaten
1 tablespoon granulated sugar, to sprinkle over
clotted cream or extra thick cream, and strawberry jam/preserves, to serve

5-cm/2-inch round fluted cookie cutter
baking sheet, lined with parchment paper

MAKES ABOUT 12

Preheat the oven to 200°C (400°F) Gas 6.

Sift the flour, baking powder and salt into a large mixing bowl. Add the butter and 'cut' it into the dry ingredients using a round-bladed knife. Then use your fingers to rub the butter into the flour until it resembles fine breadcrumbs. Add the sugar and mix to combine.

Make a well in the middle of the mixture, add the buttermilk and stir in using the knife. Once the dough starts to come together, use your hands to shape it into a rough ball. Tip it onto the work surface and very lightly knead for 30 seconds or just long enough to make the dough almost but not quite smooth – lightness of touch is key here.

Lightly dust the work surface with flour and roll out or flatten the scone dough until roughly 2 cm/¾ inch thick. Using the cookie cutter, stamp out rounds and arrange on the prepared baking sheet. Gather the dough scraps together, press into a smooth-ish ball, re-roll and stamp out more scones. Brush the top of each scone with a little of the egg white, sprinkle granulated sugar over them and bake on the middle shelf of the preheated oven for about 10 minutes or until well risen and golden brown.

Transfer the scones to a wire rack and serve still ever-so-slightly warm from the oven and most certainly on the day of making.

To serve, split the scones in half and dollop a generous spoonful of jam on the cut side of each half, then top with cream.

Chocolate scones

If you fancy a change to classic buttermilk scones (see page 116), try this recipe. Here a light sifting of cocoa powder adds a little extra indulgence to this British afternoon tea staple.

240 g/2 cups self-raising/
self-rising flour, plus extra
for dusting
25 g/2½ tablespoons cocoa
powder
1 teaspoon baking powder
a pinch of salt
75 g/5 tablespoons butter,
cut into cubes
75 g/⅔ cup caster/granulated
sugar
2 teaspoons freshly squeezed
lemon juice
160 ml/⅔ cup milk
1 egg, beaten
clotted cream or extra thick
cream, and strawberry or
raspberry jam/preserves,
to serve

5-cm/2-inch round cookie cutter

MAKES 8–10

Preheat the oven to 220°C (425°F) Gas 7 and set a large baking sheet inside the oven to heat.

Sift the flour, cocoa, baking powder and salt into a large mixing bowl. Add the butter and rub it in with your fingers, until the mixture resembles fine breadcrumbs. Stir in the sugar and make a well in the centre. Stir the lemon juice into the milk in a separate jug/pitcher, then add the liquid to the dry ingredients. Combine it quickly using a round-bladed knife – this will help to prevent over-handling the dough, which will make your scones tough.

Tip the dough out onto a lightly floured surface. Scatter a little extra flour over the dough and on your hands and lightly knead the dough. Roll or pat the dough down to make a 4-cm/ 1½-inch deep round.

Dip the cookie cutter into some flour, then plunge it into the dough – do not twist the cutter as this can affect the rise. Repeat until you can make no more scones and squidge the dough back together before patting down and cutting out some more. Brush the tops with a little beaten egg.

Carefully remove the hot baking sheet from the oven and arrange the scones on it. Bake in the preheated oven for 10–12 minutes, or until well risen.

Scones are best eaten on the day, still warm and generously smothered with clotted cream and your choice of strawberry or raspberry jam/preserves.

Pear & blackberry scone round

This delicious recipe uses ripe blackberries with seasonal pears for a rustic scone that's perfect served warm with plenty of creamy butter. A lovely autumnal treat for tea with friends.

225 g/1¾ cups self-raising/
    self-rising flour, plus extra
    for dusting
1 teaspoon baking powder
200 g/2 cups ground almonds
2 teaspoons ground cinnamon
½ teaspoon fine sea salt
115 g/1 stick butter, chilled
    and cubed
55 g/¼ cup caster/granulated
    sugar, plus extra for sprinkling
200 ml/¾ cup buttermilk
200 g/1 cup blackberries
2 ripe pears, peeled, cored and
    sliced
1 egg, beaten

*baking sheet, greased and lined
    with parchment paper*

MAKES 8 SLICES

Preheat the oven to 190°C (375°C) Gas 5.

Put the flour, baking powder, ground almonds, cinnamon and salt in a large mixing bowl and stir together.

Add the butter and rub into the flour with your fingertips, until the mixture resembles fine breadcrumbs. Add the sugar and buttermilk and mix to form a soft dough, adding a little milk if the mixture is too dry. Add the blackberries and pear slices and gently bring the dough together with your hands.

Put the dough on a floured work surface and shape it into a 23-cm/9-inch diameter round. Transfer to the prepared baking sheet using a large spatula. Brush the scone round with the beaten egg and sprinkle with a little extra sugar. Using a sharp knife, score the top of the scone into 8 sections but do not cut all the way through the dough.

Bake in the preheated oven for 20–25 minutes, until golden brown and the scone sounds hollow when you tap it on the base. Serve warm with butter.

This scone round is best eaten on the day it is made.

Yogurt bundt cake with fresh berries

This is such a simple cake, but by using a decorative bundt pan, dusting with icing/confectioner's sugar and filling the central hollow with berries, the cake comes to life. The cake has extra yogurt added to the batter to make it nice and moist. Serve with each slice of cake with whipped cream on the side.

280 g/2½ sticks butter, softened, plus extra for greasing
280 g/1½ cups caster/ granulated sugar
5 eggs
280 g/generous 2 cups self-raising/self-rising flour, sifted
2½ teaspoons baking powder
2½ tablespoons buttermilk or sour cream
200 g/scant 1 cup Greek/ US strained plain yogurt
½ teaspoon vanilla bean powder or 1 teaspoon vanilla extract
icing/confectioner's sugar, for dusting
fresh berries, to serve
double/heavy cream, whipped to stiff peaks, or crème fraîche, to serve

25-cm/10-inch bundt pan, greased

MAKES 1 CAKE

Preheat the oven to 180°C (350°F) Gas 4.

To make the cake batter, use an electric whisk to mix the butter and sugar in a bowl until light and creamy. Add the eggs and whisk again. Fold in the flour, baking powder and buttermilk or sour cream using a spatula, until incorporated. Fold the yogurt and vanilla into the cake batter using a spatula, and spoon into the prepared bundt pan.

Bake in the preheated oven for 40–50 minutes until the cake springs back to the touch and a skewer inserted into the centre of the cake comes out clean. Let cool in the pan.

Once cooled, remove from the pan by sliding a knife around the edges to loosen the cake and then inverting it onto a cake stand or plate. Dust liberally with icing/confectioner's sugar. Fill the centre of the cake with fresh berries and serve with spoonfuls of whipped cream.

This cake will store for up to 2 days in an airtight container, but should only be topped with fruit just before serving.

Tiger cake

This cake gets its name from the tiger stripes formed by the two colours of cake mixture — vanilla and chocolate. It's particularly attractive when baked in a bundt tin, so do try to get hold of one if you can.

300 g/2¾ sticks unsalted butter, softened at room temperature, plus extra for greasing
250 g/1¼ cups caster/granulated sugar
3 teaspoons vanilla extract
5 eggs
3 teaspoons baking powder
300 g/2¼ cups plain/all-purpose flour
2 tablespoons cocoa powder
1½ tablespoons double/heavy cream

23-cm/9-inch bundt pan or 18-cm/7-inch loose-bottomed/springform cake pan, greased

MAKES 1 CAKE

Preheat the oven to 180°C (350°F) Gas 4.

Put the butter and sugar in a large mixing bowl and cream with a wooden spoon or a hand-held electric whisk until pale and fluffy. Stir in the vanilla extract. Add the eggs one by one, whisking well after each addition.

In a separate bowl, sift the baking powder and flour together, then fold into the egg mixture. Spoon about one-third of the mixture into another bowl and fold in the cocoa powder and the cream.

Spoon 2 tablespoons of plain mixture into the prepared cake pan, then 1 tablespoon of chocolate mixture. Alternate in this way until you have used all the mixture and the two colours are spread randomly through the cake pan. Level the top with the back of the spoon.

Bake in the preheated oven for 50–60 minutes, until the cake is firm to the touch and a skewer inserted into the centre comes out clean.

The cake tastes best the day after baking and is also suitable for freezing.

Nordic banana cake

This banana cake recipe is packed with the spices that typify Nordic baking: ginger, cardamom and cinnamon. Throw in some ground cloves and really ripe bananas and you have a delicious and very easy cake for any time of day.

150 g/1¼ sticks unsalted butter, softened, plus extra for greasing
250 g/1¼ cups caster/granulated sugar
2 eggs
2 teaspoons baking powder
1 teaspoon salt
1 teaspoon ground ginger
2 teaspoons cardamom seeds, crushed with a pestle and mortar
2 teaspoons ground cinnamon
1 teaspoon ground cloves
300 g/2¼ cups plain/all-purpose flour
5 ripe bananas, mashed

23-cm/9-inch bundt pan or 22-cm/ 8¾-inch loose-bottomed/ springform cake pan, greased

MAKES 1 CAKE

Preheat the oven to 180°C (350°F) Gas 4.

Put the butter and sugar in a large mixing bowl and mix well. Add the eggs one by one, whisking well after each addition.

In a separate bowl, sift the baking powder, salt, spices and flour together, then fold into the egg mixture. Finally, add the mashed bananas and mix well.

Spoon the mixture into the prepared cake pan and level the top with the back of the spoon.

Bake in the preheated oven for 1 hour 20 minutes, or until a skewer inserted into the centre comes out clean. The cake tastes even better a day or two after baking and is also suitable for freezing.

Mini blueberry bundts

Topped with a blueberry drizzle and fresh berries, these tiny bundts are almost too cute to eat! Remember that with bundt pans of any size, it is important to grease the pans well so that the cakes release and don't become stuck to the fluted edges.

60 g/⅓ cup caster/granulated
    sugar
60 g/4 tablespoons butter, plus
    extra for greasing
1 egg
60 g/½ cup self-raising/self-rising
    flour
1 teaspoon baking powder
60 g/½ cup blueberries, quartered
finely grated zest of 2 lemons

BLUEBERRY DRIZZLE
250 g/2½ cups blueberries
freshly squeezed juice of 2 lemons
150 g/¾ cup caster/granulated
    sugar

*24 x 7-cm/2¾-inch mini bundt
    pans, greased*

MAKES 24

Preheat the oven to 180°C (350°F) Gas 4.

Put the sugar and butter in a mixing bowl and beat together until light and creamy, then whisk in the egg. Sift in the flour and baking powder and gently fold in, along with the quartered blueberries and lemon zest. Spoon the mixture into the prepared pans.

Bake in the preheated oven for 12–15 minutes, until the cakes spring back to your touch. Remove from the pans and let cool on a wire rack.

To make the blueberry drizzle, cut 50 g/½ cup of the blueberries in half and put them in a pan with the lemon juice. Heat gently until the blueberries are very soft and have released their juices. Strain through a sieve/strainer, pressing down on the fruit to release all the juices. Return the strained juice to the pan, add the sugar and stir over the heat until the sugar is dissolved. Drizzle over the cakes and fill the central holes of the cakes with the remaining fresh blueberries to serve.

The undrizzled cakes will keep in an airtight container for 2 days.

Crunchy prune & vanilla custard brioche cakes

These individual cakes have an indulgent fruity custard hiding under their crunchy topping. They are also good made with limoncello instead of the brandy, or leave out the alcohol altogether if you prefer. Use the thick custard you can buy in cartons from the supermarket, and if time is really short, use muffin cases instead of making your own liners. These are best eaten on the day they are made.

2 large UK/extra large US eggs

2 tablespoons Armagnac or other brandy

4 tablespoons demerara/turbinado sugar

250 g/1 cup thick ready-made custard and ½ teaspoon vanilla extract OR 2 x 120-ml/4-oz. vanilla pudding snack cups

75 g/5 tablespoons butter, plus extra for greasing

200 g/6½ oz. brioche

100 g/⅔ cup pitted, soft Agen prunes, snipped into small pieces

6-hole muffin pan, each hole well buttered and lined with a 17-cm/7-inch square of parchment paper

MAKES 6

Preheat the oven to 180°C (350°F) Gas 4.

In a mixing bowl and using a balloon whisk, whisk together the eggs, Armagnac, 1 tablespoon of the sugar, the vanilla and the custard/vanilla pudding cups.

Melt the butter in a small pan and pour into a large mixing bowl. Cut the brioche into 1–cm/½-inch squares. Toss the squares in the melted butter with 2 tablespoons of the sugar, mixing well. Divide half the squares between the parchment-lined holes in the muffin pan, pressing them down firmly to make a base.

Divide the prune pieces between each muffin, then do the same with the egg mixture. Now add the rest of the brioche squares to the muffins, piling it up high. Scatter the remaining sugar over the top.

Bake in the preheated oven for 35 minutes, or until set and golden on top. Eat warm or cold.

Fresh orange cake

This an easy to make all-in-one loaf cake flavoured with fresh orange. Look out for an unwaxed or organic orange, as half of it will be whizzed up in a processor, and the other half used for the topping.

1 orange
175 g/1½ sticks unsalted butter, very soft, plus extra for greasing
250 g/1¼ cups caster/granulated sugar
3 large UK/extra large US eggs, at room temperature
250 g/2 cups self-raising/self-rising flour
1 teaspoon bicarbonate of soda/baking soda
100 ml/scant ½ cup milk
3 tablespoons plain yogurt (not fat-free)
3 tablespoons granulated sugar, for the topping

900-g/2-lb. loaf pan, greased and lined with baking parchment

MAKES 1 CAKE

Preheat the oven to 180°C (350°F) Gas 4.

Cut the orange in half, reserving one half for the topping. Remove the pips from the other half, then cut it into 8 pieces. Put the pieces (skin still on) in a food processor and blitz until the orange is chopped into very small pieces. Transfer the orange mixture to a large mixing bowl.

Add the butter and sugar to the mixing bowl and break in the eggs. Sift the flour and bicarbonate of soda/baking soda into the bowl. Add the milk and yogurt, then beat with a wooden spoon or a hand-held electric mixer (on low speed) for 1 minute until well mixed and there are no streaks of flour visible. Spoon the mixture into the prepared pan.

Bake in the preheated oven for about 50 minutes, until a good golden brown and a skewer inserted into the centre of the cake comes out clean.

Meanwhile, make the topping. Squeeze the juice from the reserved orange half, add to a small bowl with the sugar and stir to make a thick, syrupy glaze.

Remove the loaf from the oven and stand the pan on a wire rack. Prick the top of the loaf all over with a skewer to make lots of small holes. Spoon the orange syrup all over the top so it trickles into the holes. Leave until completely cold before removing the cake from the pan, peeling off the lining paper and slicing.

Carrot cake

This carrot cake recipe uses brown sugar to provide a caramel flavour and yogurt to keep it moist and zingy. This is a dense cake and needs the freshness of the cream cheese frosting to balance the heaviness.

270 g/2 cups finely grated carrots
325 g/generous 1½ cups soft brown/light muscovado sugar
325 g/scant 2½ cups self-raising/self-rising flour
325 g/1⅜ cups sunflower oil, plus extra for oiling
5 eggs
2 tablespoons five-spice powder
grated zest of 2 lemons
1 teaspoon bicarbonate of soda/baking soda
2 tablespoons boiling water
100 g/scant ½ cup natural/plain yogurt

FROSTING
50 g/3½ tablespoons butter, softened
200 g/scant 1½ cups icing/confectioner's sugar
200 g/scant 1 cup cream cheese
grated or pared zest of 1 lemon (optional)

25-cm/10-inch round, deep cake pan, lightly oiled and lined with parchment paper

MAKES 1 CAKE

Preheat the oven to 140°C (280°F) Gas 1.

Add all the cake ingredients except the bicarbonate of soda/baking soda, boiling water and yogurt to a large mixing bowl. Fold together to combine into a smooth mixture.

Mix the bicarbonate of soda/baking soda with the boiling water until it is dissolved, then add to the mixture and fold together.

Finally add the yogurt and fold to combine all of the ingredients. Pour the mixture into the prepared cake pan.

Bake in the preheated oven for 35–40 minutes, until a skewer inserted into the centre comes out clean. Leave the cake to cool for at least 20 minutes in the cake pan, covering it with a clean kitchen towel while cooling; this slows the cooling down period to ensure a good rise but also a moist cake.

Once the cake has cooled enough so that it can be touched comfortably, remove it from the pan and finish cooling on a wire rack.

For the frosting, mix the butter and icing/confectioner's sugar in a stand mixer (or in a large bowl using a hand-held electric whisk) until fully combined. Add the cream cheese, a spoonful at a time, ensuring that the cream cheese is fully combined before adding more. Making the frosting this way avoids it becoming too soft and watery.

Frost the cake generously and decorate with some grated or pared lemon zest to finish.

This cake will keep for a couple of days, but is best eaten immediately.

Dorset apple cake

This rustic cake is moist, homely and irresistible. There are as many recipes for Dorset apple cake as there are Dorset bakers, but it is said that apple cakes with 'Dorset' in the title must never include spice, so leave your cinnamon and nutmeg in the spice rack for another time. This version has a crunchy topping of demerara/turbinado sugar and a subtle zing of lemon to complement the apples.

400 g/14 oz. apples (Bramleys, or something similarly crisp, sharp and sweet)

zest and freshly squeezed juice of 1 lemon

250 g/2 sticks unsalted butter, softened, plus extra for greasing

250 g/1¼ cups light muscovado sugar

4 eggs

50 g/⅓ cup ground almonds

a pinch of salt

250 g/2 cups self-raising/self-rising flour

2 teaspoons baking powder

1 tablespoon demerara/turbinado sugar

23-cm/9-inch round cake pan, greased and lined with parchment paper

MAKES 1 CAKE

Preheat the oven to 180°C (350°F) Gas 4.

Core and chop the apples into roughly 1-cm/½-inch pieces and toss them in the lemon juice to prevent browning.

Cream the butter and sugar together in a large mixing bowl until pale and fluffy. Beat the eggs and gradually add them to the sugar and butter mixture, whisking thoroughly between each addition. If the mixture starts to curdle, add a tablespoon of the flour. Whisk in the ground almonds and salt. Sift over the flour and baking powder, then fold them into the mixture until fully combined.

Drain the apple pieces and add them to the batter, along with the lemon zest, and fold through until the apple is evenly distributed. Pour into the prepared pan, smooth over the top with a palette knife and scatter over an even layer of demerara/turbinado sugar.

Bake in the preheated oven for 1–1¼ hours, or until a skewer inserted into the centre comes out clean. Leave the cake to cool completely in its pan on top of a wire rack before turning out.

Apple & amaretto cake

This cake is quick to make and can be left to bake while you get on with other things. It freezes well and is delicious as is; for added indulgence, whipped cream mixed with a little icing/confectioner's sugar and almond-flavoured Amaretto makes a heavenly accompaniment.

450 g/1 lb. dessert apples
350 g/2⅔ cups plain/all-purpose flour, sifted
1 tablespoon baking powder
2 teaspoons ground cinnamon
200 g/1¾ sticks butter, softened and cubed, plus extra for greasing
150 g/¾ cup light muscovado or light brown soft sugar
2 large UK/extra large US eggs
100 ml/7 tablespoons milk
100 ml/7 tablespoons amaretto
200 g/1½ cups sultanas/golden raisins

TO DECORATE
3 small, red-skinned dessert apples
2 tablespoons runny honey

23-cm/9-inch springform cake pan, 6 cm/2½ inches deep, lightly greased and base-lined with parchment paper

MAKES 1 CAKE

Preheat the oven to 180°C (350°F) Gas 4.

Core, peel and chop the apples into 1-cm/½-inch chunks.

Tip the flour, baking powder, cinnamon, butter, sugar, eggs, milk and amaretto into the bowl of a stand mixer (or use a large mixing bowl and a hand-held electric whisk) and beat together until combined.

Using a large metal spoon, thoroughly stir in the chopped apples and the sultanas/golden raisins. Spoon the mixture into the prepared pan and spread it evenly with a spatula.

To decorate, quarter the 3 red-skinned dessert apples. Don't peel them, but core them and thinly slice the quarters. Arrange the slices on top of the cake batter in slightly overlapping concentric circles.

Put the pan on a baking sheet and bake in the preheated oven for 1½–1¾ hours, or until risen and golden, a skewer inserted into the centre comes out clean and the apple slices on top are burnished. Cover the cake with foil towards the end of cooking to prevent over-browning, if necessary.

Warm the honey in a small pan, then use to brush over the top of the cake. Leave to cool in the pan before releasing it, peeling off the base paper and transferring to a serving plate.

Kladdkaka

This very easy Swedish chocolate mud cake has a sticky, gooey centre and is delicious served with whipped cream.

2 eggs
300 g/1½ cups caster/granulated
    sugar
65 g/½ cup plain/all-purpose flour
40 g/⅓ cup cocoa powder, plus
    extra for dusting
a pinch of salt
2 teaspoons vanilla extract
1 tablespoon dark rum
115 g/1 stick butter, melted,
    plus extra for greasing
ice cream or whipped cream,
    to serve

*20-cm/8-inch round pie plate,
    greased*

MAKES 1 CAKE

Preheat the oven to 150°C (300°F) Gas 2.

Crack the eggs into a mixing bowl and add the sugar. Sift in the dry ingredients and whisk. Add the vanilla, rum and melted butter and whisk to combine. Pour the batter into the prepared pie plate.

Bake in the preheated oven for 30–35 minutes. The cake will still be very gooey in the middle. Serve hot with vanilla ice cream or leave to cool and serve with whipped cream, dusted with cocoa powder.

Index

Recipe credits

Victoria Glass
Blueberry muffins
Chocolate & beetroot mini loaf cakes
Chocolate scones
Dorset apple cake
Double chocolate chip muffins
Lemon drizzle loaf cake
Kladdkaka
Rock cakes

Sarah Randall
Apple & amaretto cake
Banana & passion fruit loaf
Beetroot, cherry & chocolate cakes
Crunchy prune & vanilla custard
  brioche cakes
Crunchy-topped raspberry & banana
  muffins
Mocha swirl loaf with espresso icing
Mulled wine & cranberry tea bread
Toffee pear muffins

Julian Day
Apricot & nut loaf
Banana & walnut bread
Bara brith
Carrot loaf cake
Chocolate & pecan muffins
Fruit bread
Lavender loaf

Hannah Miles
Pear & blackberry scone round
Gluten-free banana & brazil nut bread
Gluten-free lemon & amaretto loaf
  cakes
Mini blueberry bundts
Yogurt bundt cake with fresh berries

Mat Follas
Carrot cake
Chocolate & vanilla marble cake
Sticky gingerbread loaf

Miisa Mink
Nordic banana cake
Oatbake with blueberries & raspberries
Tiger cake

Shelagh Ryan
Banana bread with raspberry labne
Lemon polenta cakes
Sticky toffee ginger loaf

Clare Burnet
Blueberry muffins with lemon & white
  chocolate
Chocolate & banana muffins

Maxine Clark
Chocolate, cherry & macadamia tea
  breads
Chocolate, yogurt & banana tea bread

Dunja Gulin
Vegan rich tea bread
Vegan sweet potato pound cake

Victoria Hall
Gluten-free lemon & poppy seed
  drizzle loaf
Gluten-free 'malt' loaf

Lola's Cupcakes
Castella cake
Classic banana bread

Suzy Pelta
Caramel banana mug cake
Cream cheese coffee cake muffins

Annie Rigg
Buttermilk scones
Pain d'épices

Wendy Sweetser
Cornish saffron cake
Iced orange seed cake

Kiki Bee
Tea bread, Long Island style

Susannah Blake
Sticky marzipan & cherry loaf

Linda Collister
Fresh orange cake

Megan Davies
Peanut butter banana bread

Amy Ruth Finegold
Almond flour tea loaf with fresh
  berries

Tonia George
Chocolate chip banana bread

Tori Haschka
Latte banana bread

Claire & Lucy McDonald
Choc-chip banana bread in a jar

Isidora Popovic
Lemon loaf with white chocolate
  frosting

Photo credits

Martin Brigdale
Page 77

Peter Cassidy
Pages 17, 41, 45, 73, 125, 126

Jonathon Gregson
Pages 14, 95, 98–99

Dan Jones
Pages 3, 96, 111, 118, 141

Adrian Lawrence
Pages 30, 49, 82, 103

Lisa Linder
Page 85

William Lingwood
Pages 62, 129

Steve Painter
Pages 10, 21, 34, 42, 53, 57, 69, 74,
78, 81, 91, 122, 134

William Reavell
Pages 1, 22, 104, 121

Stuart West
Pages 29, 50, 54

Kate Whittaker
Pages 2, 13, 25, 37, 38, 66, 92, 100,
107, 108, 117, 130, 138

Isobel Wield
Pages 18, 46, 89, 114, 137

Claire Winfield
Pages 6, 26, 58, 65, 70

Polly Wreford
Page 133